WALKING the RIDGES of LAKELAND

WALKING the RIDGES of LAKELAND

according to WAINWRIGHT'S PICTORIAL GUIDES *Books 1–3*

BOB ALLEN

with PETER LINNEY

MICHAEL JOSEPH
LONDON

MICHAEL JOSEPH LTD

Published by the Penguin Group
27 Wrights Lane, London W8 5TZ
Viking Penguin Inc., 375 Hudson Street, New York, New York 10014, USA
Penguin Books Australia Ltd, Ringwood, Victoria, Australia
Penguin Books Canada Ltd, 10 Alcorn Avenue, Toronto, Ontario, Canada M4V 3B2
Penguin Books (NZ) Ltd, 182–190 Wairau Road, Auckland 10, New Zealand

Penguin Books Ltd, Registered Offices: Harmondsworth, Middlesex, England

First published in Great Britain 1995

Typeset by Cambridge Photosetting Services
Colour reproduction by Saxon Photolitho Ltd.
Printed in Great Britain by Butler & Tanner, Frome and London

A CIP catalogue record for this book is available from the British Library

ISBN 0 7181 3877 5

Half-title page: Thornthwaite Beacon, with Windermere in the distance.
Title page: The Ill Bell ridge seen from the Kirkstone Pass road.
Endpapers: Short Stile and Twopenny Crag from the slope of High Street.

CONTENTS

  ★ traverse

PREFACE

by PETER LINNEY

There have been very few occasions in my life when I have sensed that I was at a moment of discovery, that something special was round the corner. One such occasion was during the early development work for *The Official Wainwright Gazetteer*, and it was a moment for which I was quite unprepared.

Most fellwalkers – and especially AW – recognise the exhilaration of walking the ridges between mountains, and the joy of keeping to high ground having once achieved it. When I find I am losing ground, I often mutter the old adage to myself: 'High ground once taken should not be readily yielded.'

AW identified no fewer than 318 ridge routes between the 181 Lakeland fells which have ridge connections (33 of the 214 fells described in the seven Pictorial Guides have no stated connection with a neighbouring fell). I drew my first map indicating the position of the 214 fells as far back as 1982 and when I started gathering information for the *Gazetteer*, my engineering training nagged at me to look at the presentation of the information. This led me to add the 178 starting points specifically indicated or hinted at by AW in the guidebooks, together with the ascents to the fells shown as straight dotted lines. When I came to consider the ridge routes, which AW detailed at the end of his descriptions of the relevant fells, I added these to the maps in the form of solid straight lines connecting the appropriate fells.

It was at this point that my excitement reached boiling point for I saw in front of me a network of routes up, down and across Lakeland which quite took my breath away; I saw ideas for ridge walks which had never before occurred to me.

Turning these ideas into a book containing the best ridge walks was clearly a job for 'the professionals' and so it was with much anticipation that Jenny Dereham, the Wainwright editor, arranged for me to meet one of her other authors, Bob Allen – the experienced and accomplished climber, walker, photographer and writer. Bob's reaction at seeing the map was similar to my own, and to others who have since seen it; conversation ceased as minds already filled with Lakeland mountain knowledge saw new routes as well as reliving old favourites. I was delighted when Bob agreed to write the route descriptions and prepare the accompanying photographs in this first volume of the ridges of Lakeland according to Wainwright.

Stickle Tarn, Harrison Stickle and Pavey Ark from near Blea Rigg.

INTRODUCTION

I will freely admit that I am a late convert to Wainwright. As a young man I saw the fells of Lakeland almost exclusively as a rock-climbing playground and fellwalking something that was necessary to get to the crags, or to be enjoyed only when it was not possible to climb on the crags. What little I knew of AW's Pictorial Guides (and I had bought two or three of them in the sixties and early seventies but had not really looked at them in detail) had left with me the impression of fussiness. Worse, I was impatient of what I thought was AW's attitude seeming to treat all crags as fearsome places to be avoided. Yet I was climbing all over those fearsome places!

With age came a little more wisdom. I realised that just being in the mountains, whether climbing, walking, running or skiing, was what mattered. I found an increasing satisfaction in trying to capture the marvellous Lake District landscape on film. And I realised that AW's achievement was a most remarkable one, which nobody else could ever hope to emulate.

Even so, when Jenny Dereham (who has edited all but one of my own books and is also the editor of the Wainwright series) asked me to look at a new kind of map, drawn by a chap called Peter Linney and based on the Pictorial Guides, I still wondered what could be really *different* about it. But as soon as I saw it I realised that the network of lines linking various fells had many differences from those that I have taken for granted for thirty years. Certain ridge walks which I have considered classics, such as 'The Round of Easedale' or 'The Langdale Skyline', are *not* to be found on *this* map. Some classics are there, of course, but it was the realisation that there were numerous *unusual* ridge circuits on this map that excited me and which form the basis of this book.

There is, in fact, too much material for one book, so this is the first of two and this one covers the Eastern, Far Eastern and Central Fells, the first three of the Pictorial Guides. The book contains 23 horseshoe ridge walks starting from and finishing in the same place, plus 4 major traverses. AW covered 98 fells in those first three guidebooks and these ridge walks go over 75 of them, in the main omitting only isolated outliers. Anybody walking all the ground covered in the book, as of course I have done in order to produce the details and photographs, will cover just over 300 miles and climb almost 94,000ft/28,650m. Excluding the four long traverses, which average 19 miles, the other

23 walks average 10 miles with an average height gain of just under 3200ft/975m, so very few of them could be described as doddles.

MAPS: The walks cover distances from a few miles to over twenty and so the maps are inevitably at different scales to fit the page. The described and recommended routes on my sketch maps are shown by red pecks, but I do emphasise that my showing the pecks on the map does not always mean that there is a path on the ground, although there usually will be. When the 'main path' is mentioned in the text, that is an abbreviation for 'the most used and obvious path *on the ground*', which is not always the same as the path indicated on the Ordnance Survey map. Extra care should be taken in the summer (when high bracken can sometimes obscure paths) or, more importantly, turns.

GRADIENT PROFILES: The scale of these was decided by the desire to give the most realistic profiles possible, the one that looks most like the gradient *feels* like when you are doing it.

ROUTE CARDS/TABLES: The heights in feet listed here are those used by AW in the Pictorial Guides, but modern maps are of course metric (and not necessarily any better for that!). AW's heights and OS metric heights rarely convert exactly from one to the other and, in addition to the conversion problem, there is the complication that the OS has revised certain heights since AW wrote his guides. The metric heights given are therefore those used on the latest OS 1:25 000 maps, or an estimate where no specific height is given.

PLACE NAMES: These are generally those used by the Ordnance Survey, but just a few of the older spellings, which AW much preferred (as does this author and his editor) have been retained.

TIMES: The times given for completing any of the walks are a guide only, as there are too many variables, including weather, to be precise. They are, however, based on a consideration of AW's times, Naismith's Rule (one hour per three miles plus half an hour per one thousand feet of ascent) and my own experience of actually doing the walks. Long lunch stops are not included, short ones are.

ACCESS: There is a general acceptance of a freedom to roam on the high land of the Lake District, above the level of the intake walls. There are some areas, however, where there are restrictions on the high land also and I have made this clear in the text. I have taken great care to ensure that all routes use public rights of way (or permissive paths where rights of way are not shown on the OS maps) to get onto the high land above the intake walls. In a few cases, this means that I have had to modify some of AW's routes, but these will be obvious in the text. Compass directions are frequently given in the text and it should be obvious that the correct OS map and a compass should always be carried.

ACKNOWLEDGEMENTS

My debt to the Ordnance Survey and their wonderful maps will be obvious. Peter Linney's work in producing the Wainwright ridge-line network is, as mentioned above, the basis of this book and I would not have had the great pleasure of walking all these ridges again without it. But he is also responsible for the gradient profiles and the route cards/tables while his son Andrew has done the graphic work necessary for those and has in addition put all the place names on my maps.

Jenny Dereham has, as always, made the finished production so much better than it might have been. The direct quotations from the Pictorial Guides to the Lake District are reproduced with kind permission of Michael Joseph Ltd. The area managers of the Lake District National Park have been unfailingly helpful over matters of access and I have been glad of their advice.

On the fells, my old friend Roger Bowers has insisted on walking as much as possible with me; Ernest Shepherd (despite being nearly eighty years of age) has given me welcome support; Rob Rose and his family have done the same, while my canine pals Henry and Freddie have covered every inch. I am grateful to them all.

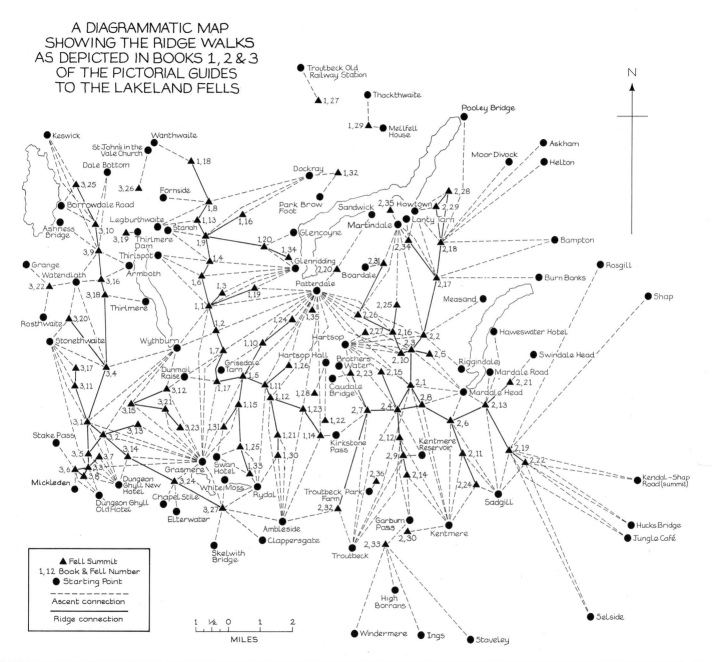

A DIAGRAMMATIC MAP
SHOWING THE RIDGE WALKS
AS DEPICTED IN BOOKS 1, 2 & 3
OF THE PICTORIAL GUIDES
TO THE LAKELAND FELLS

N

▲ Fell Summit
1,12 Book & Fell Number
● Starting Point

- - - - - Ascent connection

———— Ridge connection

1 ½ 0 1 2
MILES

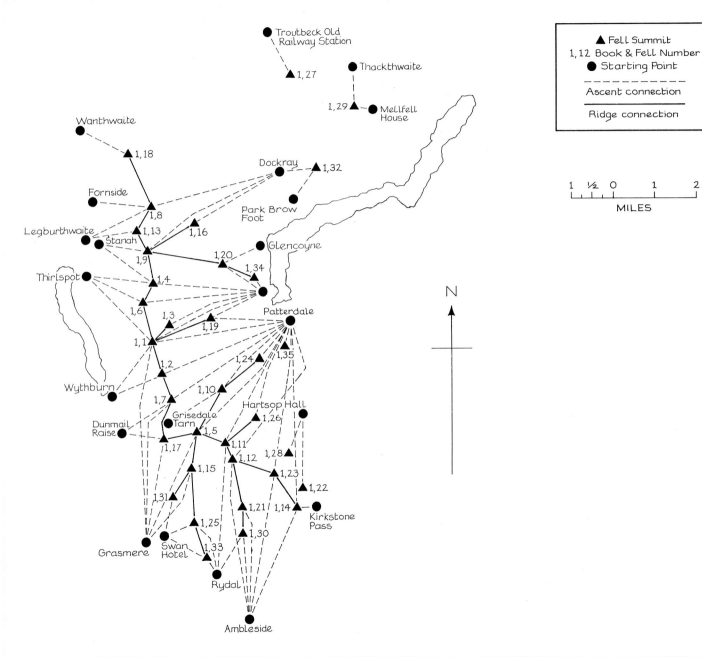

Troutbeck Old Railway Station

▲1,27

Thackthwaite

1,29▲● Mellfell House

Wanthwaite

▲1,18

Fornside

Dockray ▲1,32

▲1,8

Park Brow Foot

▲1,13

▲1,16

Legburthwaite

▲1,9

Stanah

1,20

Glencoyne

▲1,34

Thirlspot

▲1,4

Patterdale

1,6

▲1,3

▲1,19

1,1

▲

1,2

1,24 ▲

1,35

Wythburn

1,10

1,7 ▲

Hartsop Hall

Grisedale Tarn

1,26

Dunmail Raise

1,5

1,17

1,11

1,28 ▲

1,15

1,12

1,23

1,31 ▲

1,22

1,21

1,14 ▲

Kirkstone Pass

1,25

1,30

Grasmere

Swan Hotel

1,33

Rydal

Ambleside

N

▲ Fell Summit
1,12 Book & Fell Number
● Starting Point
------- Ascent connection
Ridge connection

1 ½ 0 1 2
MILES

PART ONE

THE EASTERN FELLS

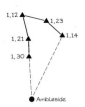

Ambleside

1 THE SCANDALE SKYLINE

Best Map: *OS 1:25000 Outdoor Leisure 7, South Eastern area*
Approximate time: *5½–6 hours*
Terrain: *Good paths, sometimes peaty in the first half; mixed ground and then good paths for most of the return.*

ITINERARY	Book & Fell No	Height of ascent	Distance	Cumulative distance	Height above sea level	
		feet	miles	miles	feet	mtrs
AMBLESIDE					250	76
Low Pike	1.30	1500	2.25	2.25	1657	508
High Pike	1.21	600	0.67	2.92	2155	656
Dove Crag	1.12	470	1.00	3.92	2603	792
Little Hart Crag	1.23	200	1.25	5.17	2091	637
Red Screes	1.14	900	1.25	6.42	2541	776
AMBLESIDE			4.00	10.42	250	76
Totals of heights and distances		3670	10.42			

This enjoyable circuit has some wonderful scenic highlights and is a good example of the pleasures of walking on the eastern fells of Lakeland. Scandale drains to Windermere and so Ambleside is the obvious starting point, the Rydal Road car park being the most convenient (grid ref 376047).

From the car park, cross the A591 to the Kirkstone Road opposite, then turn immediately left up 'Nook Lane' (its correct spelling, whatever additional letters may have been added by scrawlers). The metalled lane leads gently uphill but becomes a track beyond Nook End Farm, quickly leading to the crossing of Scandale Beck by Low Sweden Bridge. Here the water pours in splashing cascades down a wooded gill and the grassy track swings back right above and beside the gill, winding up pleasant sheep pastures until it passes through a third gateway.

There is a choice of ways now, although they shortly rejoin. Those wishing to walk every yard of the ridge will trend left to a path beside the ridge-top wall and follow it

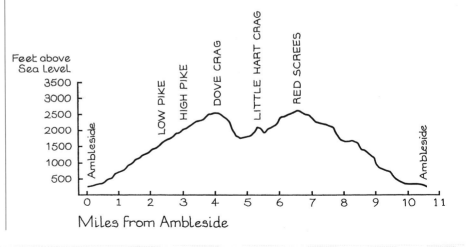

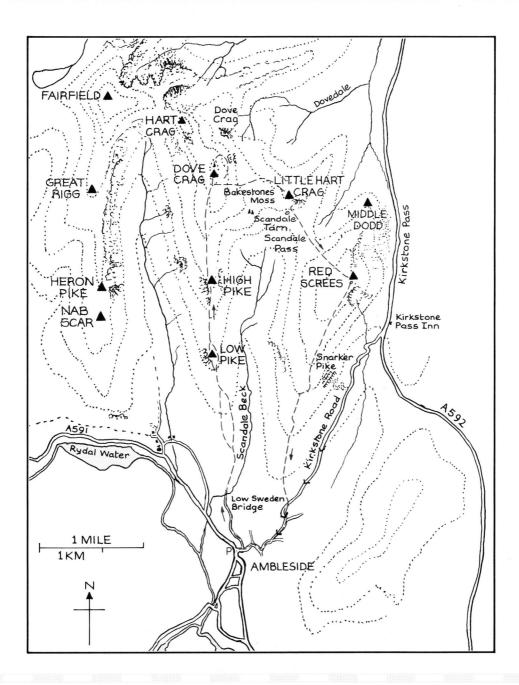

FAIRFIELD ▲

HART
CRAG ▲

Dove
Crag

Dovedale

GREAT
RIGG ▲

DOVE
CRAG ▲

LITTLE HART
▲ CRAG

Bakestones
Moss

MIDDLE
DODD ▲

Scandale
Tarn

Scandale
Pass

Kirkstone Pass

HERON
PIKE ▲

▲ HIGH
PIKE

RED
SCREES ▲

NAB
SCAR ▲

Kirkstone
Pass Inn

▲ LOW
PIKE

Snarker
Pike

A592

Scandale Beck

Kirkstone Road

A591

Rydal Water

Low Sweden
Bridge

1 MILE

1 KM

P

AMBLESIDE

N

religiously to an obstacle in the form of a worn rock step about 10ft high. AW noted that 'The step is not difficult to climb if the right foot is used first, the right foot in this case being the left.' If you are still left looking for the right way after trying this, try easier rocks on the right instead. Walkers not wishing to muddle up their rights with their lefts will stay on the main path. This continues across more pleasant pastures to another gateway by a sheepfold, then rises more steeply up brackeny slopes towards some belts of rock. These are Low and High Brock Crags, both low enough to be colonized by trees, and the path winds up their different levels until it meets the ridge-top wall. (Walkers who followed the wall all the way will join here.)

Ahead now rises Low Pike, its shape clearly defined and with the wall running over its crest. The path by-passes its rocky top on the right, but do not fail to cut back left on a little path leading no more than 30ft higher to its summit, as it is a splendid viewpoint for the ridge ahead and, indeed, up the length of Scandale. In 1954, AW noted that 'There is no cairn nor room for one' but there is one there now.

Rejoining the path, this continues over increasingly steeper ground and then climbs up the first of several bands of rock outcropping on the ridge towards the next top rearing up ahead, that of High Pike. On the way it is impossible not to be aware of the adjacent wall, not just because the path is so close beside it, but because it is so solidly constructed, in horizontal courses up steeply sloping rock; there is hardly a breach in it. A marvellous example of a declining skill that has fashioned our landscape for centuries.

High Pike, despite its imposing rocky appearance from below, proves to have an almost flat and grassy top. There is a cairn on a small crag, but no other rocks apart from those of the wall itself, still stoutly standing alongside. Rock is indeed now left behind as the ridge flattens into a broad plateau, and the path rises on grass at a gentle angle and over patches of spongy peat, making fast progress towards the next objective which is Dove Crag.

Reaching a point where the wall makes a slight but definite elbow bend to the left it is notable how, after showing such remarkable strength, it suddenly collapses within sight of the top and it is the tumbledown version which accompanies the ridge path up the last easy slope. A cairn found on some flat rocks just to the right of the wall marks the actual top of Dove Crag. There is little of interest in the view from here to detain anybody, but Dove Crag is worth more exploration than this. About 100 yards away to the north, in an area of many stones, is another cairn, and from this one are grand views to Helvellyn, to St Sunday Crag, to Fairfield, to High Street, to Place Fell and down Dovedale to Ullswater. But you still gain little idea of the sheer size and overhanging nature of the great cliff of Dove Crag itself, one of the finest rock-climbing arenas in the Lake District, which buttresses this bland summit. A truer impression of its size will shortly be gained on the descent that follows towards Scandale Pass.

Return to the wall and reverse steps to the south, passing the summit cairn again and

heading for High Pike. But in about 300 yards down the first gentle slope beyond the cairn, watch for where a line of iron and wooden fence posts turns off at right-angles, to the east. A footpath follows this line of posts faithfully down easy grass slopes, then down rougher ground and out onto the easier level of Bakestones Moss. Look to your left on this descent and you will see at least something of the real Dove Crag.

In describing the ascent of Dove Crag from Patterdale (Dove Crag 4), AW says: 'It is believed that Hunsett Cove was once the crater of a volcano.' I have climbed on Dove Crag several times (thrice on a route called Hangover, which is to do with the angle of the cliff rather than my condition at the time) and can well believe that the chaotic area of boulders below the great cliff, which AW calls Hunsett Cove, may well have volcanic origins. But the name Hunsett Cove itself is a puzzle. The only one like it that I can find on any of my editions of the OS maps is Houndshope Cove, but that is clearly shown

The ridge rising to High Pike and Dove Crag.

further on, between Dove Crag and Hart Crag. I leave the puzzle to others better qualified than me to solve.

Beyond Bakestones Moss the next objective is Little Hart Crag. The path towards it stays with the line of fence-posts as they turn sharp right and continue along the high land above the upper reaches of Dovedale, on the left, becoming less obvious over some rough grass and boggy stretches, but never in doubt. It does, however, turn away from Little Hart Crag towards a wall rising from Scandale Pass, so you need to divert from the path to enjoy an easy scramble onto this fine double-topped crag, where there is a little cairn on a rock ledge at the west end and which has several short but steep rock faces. Its commanding position at the head of Scandale makes it the best viewpoint for the valley and I once watched a Red Arrows' aerobatic display over Windermere from here.

Leaving Little Hart Crag, regain the path beside the fence-posts and, passing the tiny Scandale Tarn on the right, complete the descent to Scandale Pass. The next top is Red Screes, and a stony slope stretches to the south-east towards it on the other side of the pass, but the summit cannot be distinguished from below. A footpath does trace a faint line in the right direction, but it is not very clear and in anything less than perfect visibility may not be seen at all. However, a wall, collapsed for much of its length but quite unmistakable, also rises up the same slope and a path has developed beside this, in places passing over slabby rocks, eventually intersecting with another wall, quite definitely collapsed, traversing the fellside. From this point upwards there is no wall, but a last short ascent in a straight line trending half-left (east) will take you to the summit ridge of Red Screes. From here you will be looking down the steep drop on the rim of a combe plunging almost to the road running through the Kirkstone Pass. Follow the path to the left around the rim to reach a large untidy cairn, the trig point, a circular windbreak and some wonderful views. That looking northwards down to and over Middle Dodd to Patterdale must be the finest, but those back towards Dove Crag and those over Caudale Moor towards High Street are scarcely less impressive.

Leaving the trig point and heading south-west, almost immediately passing a small tarn on the right, the path leads along the edge of the steep drop again to a large cairn, then down a stony slope which is crossed by the remains of a wall. Below this the rocky ground gives way to peatier passages and the path runs beside a wall on the left. The cairn marking Snarker Pike will be seen, but only if you watch for it, on the other side of this wall. Gentler slopes continue the descent but then turn more sharply down again and swing right, in a wide funnel between walls, to reach a ladder-stile at the neck of the funnel. On its far side the path leads into a walled lane curving left below some small but rugged rock outcrops, with a good view back to the High Pike ridge again on the far side of Scandale.

The downhill wall of the lane is frequently collapsed, allowing easy grassy walking outside its confines and good views across the lower part of Scandale and to Rydal, with

one more ladder-stile at a cross wall. The route remains clear and without any problems, with just one more stile to cross before veering left to reach the Kirkstone Pass Road at a gate. A right turn here and a quick descent leads back into Ambleside. Just before reaching the A591 again you will pass the doors of that excellent pub, the Golden Rule. It's a good place to relive some of the highlights of a grand walk.

High Pike seen across Scandale from near Snarker Pike.

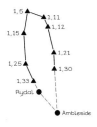

2 THE CLASSIC FAIRFIELD HORSESHOE

BEST MAP: *OS 1:50 000 Landranger 90, Penrith, Keswick & Ambleside area. At OS 1:25 000 scale both Outdoor Leisure 5, North Eastern area and Outdoor Leisure 7, South Eastern area are needed.*
APPROXIMATE TIME: *6 hours*
TERRAIN: *All on good paths, stony on Fairfield and boggy in places on the descent.*

ITINERARY	Book & Fell No	Height of ascent	Distance	Cumulative distance	Height above sea level	
		feet	miles	miles	feet	mtrs
AMBLESIDE					250	76
Rydal		0	1.50	1.50	250	76
Nab Scar	1.33	1200	1.00	2.50	1450	442
Heron Pike	1.25	570	0.67	3.17	2003	612
Great Rigg	1.15	550	1.50	4.67	2513	766
Fairfield	1.05	500	1.00	5.67	2863	873
Hart Crag	1.11	150	1.00	6.67	2698	822
Dove Crag	1.12	260	0.75	7.42	2603	792
High Pike	1.21	0	1.00	8.42	2155	656
Low Pike	1.30	100	0.67	9.09	1657	508
AMBLESIDE				2.25	11.34	250	76
Totals of heights and distances		3330	11.34			

A classic round of the eastern fells, the Fairfield Horseshoe is a tour of the fells overlooking Rydal Beck although there are several other horseshoes in which Fairfield is at least as important. The round stages one of the most popular fell races.

Starting from the Rydal Road car park in Ambleside (grid ref 376047) walk along the A591 towards Grasmere and turn right just beyond Scandale Bridge through imposing iron gates (signed for Rydal Hall). A manicured pathway leads through sylvan parkland, round the back of Rydal Hall, now a Youth Centre with a tea shop, to reach the metalled road almost opposite Rydal Mount. Turn uphill here, through a gate at the bottom of a wide walled lane and with the craggy top of Nab Scar in view directly ahead. An obvious signed path leads steeply towards it, over a ladder-stile at the edge of a larch plantation, then winding upwards round the right-hand side of the rocks ahead to join the rocky ridge about 1000ft above Rydal Water which is seen below on the left, backed by Loughrigg Fell. Here, immediately on the left of the path and just before reaching the highest rocks, is the flat square yard of stone, about 6 inches thick, marking the Thirlmere aqueduct vertically below and illustrated in the Pictorial Guide.

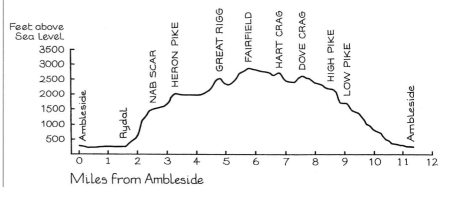

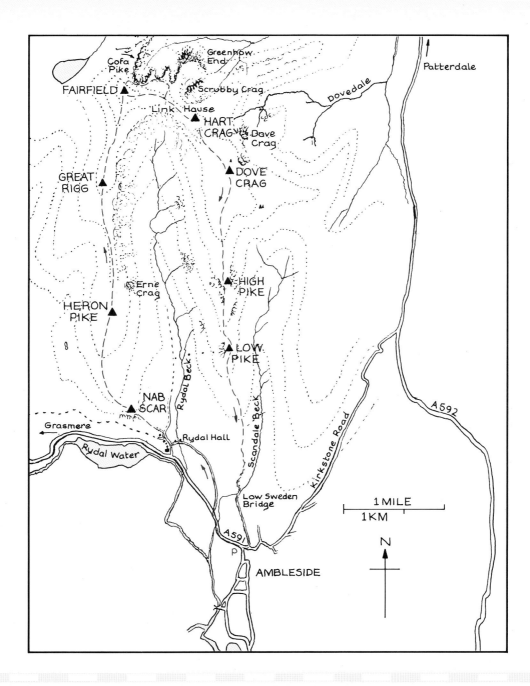

Rydal Water from the stone block on Nab Scar.

The path continues up the escarpment, crosses a wall by a ladder-stile and just beyond this, on the left of the path and next to a totally collapsed wall, is the heap of stones marking the top of Nab Scar. Its craggy south face overlooks Rydal Water but is unseen from here. The path ahead leaves the ridge to skirt rocky ground, then continues up some eroded grooves to reach a small cairn on top of a little outcrop of white quartzite: this is Heron Pike. Ahead, at last, is a fine view to Dunmail Raise and Steel Fell, to Great Rigg and Fairfield itself. Immediately beyond Heron Pike is a small depression and beyond that the ridge rises to a slightly higher but more notably rocky little peak. The ridge path bypasses this un-named top on its left, but it has a good cairn built where a pointed rock

Steel Fell and Dunmail Raise from near Heron Pike.

slab meets a wall running down left into Rydale. Just below on the Rydal side are the steeper rocks of Erne Crag. (I have no doubt that if AW had called this un-named summit 'Erne Crag Top' in his Pictorial Guide of 1955, it would have had that name by now on the OS maps.)

The path now undulates along an almost flat ridge, with a tiny pool near its lowest point, from which grass slopes on the left fall away to Greenhead Gill, while on the right steeper slopes with more scree fall to Rydale. A large cairn marks the point where a path goes off left down the subsidiary ridge to Stone Arthur but the ascent continues up broken rocks to reach another large one on Great Rigg amidst a scattering of small rocks

Great Rigg and Fairfield from just north of Heron Pike.

and some close-cropped turf. Looking back towards Windermere and Heron Pike, the obvious dark vertical gash of a gully can now be seen falling to Rydal Beck, yet walking along the ridge top from Heron Pike it is passed completely unnoticed.

A little depression follows and then the path leads upwards gradually onto Fairfield's large domed plateau, with cairns marking the way towards a circular stone shelter. The summit cairn is about 20 paces to the north-east, with a multi-chambered windbreak, a commodious des. res., 25 paces north of that, the latter in a superb position overlooking the great combes gouged by the ice out of the north face and falling to Deepdale. A little to the north-west, the slope drops sharply towards the pointed top of Cofa Pike on the descending ridge towards St Sunday Crag and from here the combes on the east face of Helvellyn are seen at their best.

A line of cairns now leads off to the south-east, almost immediately swinging east and keeping well back from the edges overlooking Deepdale. In poor weather this must be the preferred route to Link Hause and Hart Crag, as it is obvious and safe, but a narrow path skirts much closer to the edge and in clear conditions enhances the tremendous views.

AW recommends a detour to the top of Greenhow End, involving a gradual descent to the north-east, skirting the top of the great gully of Black Tippet at the left side of Hutaple Crag and revealing more superb rock scenery. Then the ground narrows to a sharp arête leading to Greenhow End (from where, incidentally, a fine scramble-walking route leads down a rock buttress to Link Cove). Rather oddly, however, AW suggests a particular point, before reaching Greenhow End, as the best place from which to view the north face of Fairfield. Yet his own fine drawing of the north face of Fairfield, which I personally think is the best view also, is from near Cofa Pike, looking in the opposite direction. A strange anomaly.

Returning to the cairned main path going south-east, a stony descent leads to Link Hause. A backward glance here reveals the vertical rock walls of Scrubby Crag, so much better than the broken little outcrops that form the north face of Hart Crag up the edge of which the path now climbs. A large pile of stones, possibly the site of a former shelter, is just left of the path at the top of the main rise and a hundred paces beyond this, on a patch of peat, a grassy cairned path leads off to the north-east. The ridge line towards Dove Crag is along the higher ground a little further right, where two cairns marking the top of Hart Crag are found. From the south cairn the skyline edges of two buttresses on Dove Crag (the crag rather than the top of the fell) are visible, as is the line of the collapsed wall rising from the depression beyond Hart Crag to the south-east up to Dove Crag's bland fell top. The path beside this wall is obvious, down a slope over big stones and then rising over grassier terrain to pass by a first cairn on the edge of an extensive area of sharp-edged stones. A stroll beyond these reveals Dovedale far below. A second cairn is a hundred paces further south on top of some flat slabby rocks, just east of the crumbling wall and is the recognized summit.

After a short descent down a slight slope to the south a line of fence posts leads out eastwards from a slight bend in the wall, which has now gathered strength and stands upright again, providing shelter from westerly winds as the main ridge path descends beside it. A gradual descent down grass, with occasional fairly boggy sections beside the wall on the right, leads over the top of the almost conical shape of High Pike. Now the descent is noticeably steeper, the wall marching along the crest of the ridge and at one point descending steeper ground down rock steps. A ladder-stile crosses a transverse wall running down towards Scandale on the approach to Low Pike but then the path turns downhill just before reaching this distinctive little upthrust on the ridge. It is, however, a good point for a retrospective view back up the ridge to High Pike and well worth a few seconds' delay to enjoy it.

For Ambleside the main way is obvious and continues alongside the wall for some distance before veering sharp left and then back right to find a way between High and Low Brock Crags. When this occurs, a direct route continues beside the wall, almost immediately reaching a vertical rock step which can be a little awkward in descent but may be by-passed on the left. This path stays beside the wall until beyond a ladder-stile when it turns down a short slope to join with the main path again. This has joined a pleasantly grassy cart track winding down through sheep pastures, through several gateways, to cross Scandale Beck at Low Sweden Bridge and turn into Nook Lane. Beyond Nook End Farm the track is metalled and this completes the return to Ambleside, emerging, with anticipation, into Kirkstone Road almost opposite the Golden Rule pub.

1,15
1,31
1,25
Grasmere, Swan Hotel

3 THE GREENHEAD GILL ROUND

BEST MAP: *OS 1:25 000 Outdoor Leisure 7, South Eastern area*
APPROXIMATE TIME: *About 3¼ hours*
TERRAIN: *Mostly on good firm paths, but some of the descent is trackless over grass.*

ITINERARY	Book & Fell No	Height of ascent	Distance	Cumulative distance	Height above sea level	
		feet	miles	miles	feet	mtrs
GRASMERE, SWAN HOTEL					250	76
Stone Arthur	1.31	1400	1.00	1.00	1652	504
Great Rigg	1.15	860	1.25	2.25	2513	766
Heron Pike	1.25	150	1.50	3.75	2003	612
GRASMERE, SWAN HOTEL			1.25	5.00	250	76
Totals of heights and distances		2410	5.00			

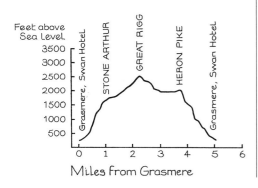

This round gives a short but fairly stiff gallop suitable for a half day or so, and since all the slopes face roughly south they can expect to receive any available sun. The views over the vale of Grasmere are attractive but by no means the only ones.

Start from Grasmere; the large car park at the north end may be the most convenient but it is a popular tourist village and a search may be necessary. Now walk north up the B5287 to its junction with the A591; the Swan Hotel is in the corner opposite. Go up the lane beside the Swan, past the first side road on the right to the second, a narrow metalled drive signed 'Public footpath Greenhead Gill, Allcock Tarn'. At its end is a gate onto open fell and a path signed 'Stone Arthur'. This climbs steeply beside a wall on the left, with acres of bracken, immensely tall in high summer, stretching up the slopes ahead, to the top corner of a wooded enclosure. Here it swings back sharp right, crosses an unnamed little gill and, at an easier gradient, slants across the fellside beside traces of wall to reach a broad spur overlooking Greenhead Gill. Here the path turns left up the spur, soon leaving the bracken behind, and then takes the easiest line to where the spur steepens into an outcrop of short rock walls crowned by a compact rock summit.

This is Stone Arthur, only an incident on the long ridge from Great Rigg, but a romantic might associate the rocks with a castle and thus with Arthurian legend. AW said there was no cairn here; that omission was rectified long ago. In the right light it is probably true that 'the gem of the view is Easedale Tarn in its wild setting among colourful fells', although Alcock Tarn on its rocky shelf is most attractive when it just catches the evening light.

Beyond a slight depression the ridge rises again, shortly passing a solid roofless square stone shelter, the space inside which would just allow a single person to sit in it, like a loo with a view. Rising over grass between occasional outcrops there is indeed little change in the view until the last dip before the pull up to Great Rigg. Then Striding Edge on Helvellyn becomes visible through the notch between Fairfield and Dolly-waggon Pike, and Seat Sandal is seen across Tongue Gill on the left. Grooves in more grass slopes lead to a junction with the main ridge at a large cairn, with the ground drop-

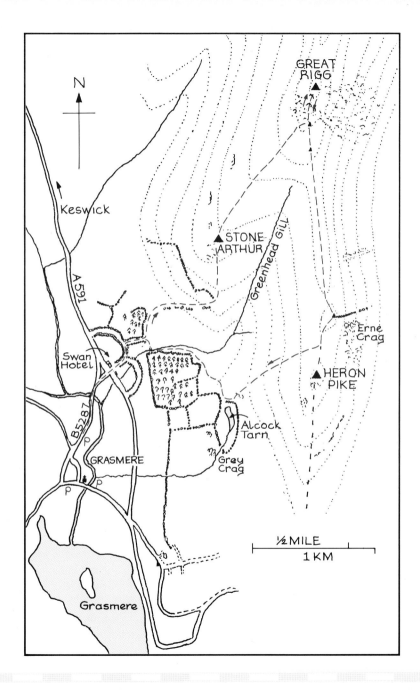

Stone Arthur and Great Rigg seen from Grasmere.

ping steeply away into Stone Cove beyond. A left turn up the rocks which outcrop on the ridge here, passing another cairn, leads shortly to a much bigger one in a scattering of rocks amidst some close-cropped turf: this is Great Rigg. Some of the turf is still in good order but I doubt that, as AW suggested, 'many a cricket-ground would welcome' it any more.

The rising ridge continues to Fairfield, but our route turns downhill, reversing the last bit of the ascent to a depression from where more steep grass slopes sweep down into Greenhead Gill on the right. An almost level path follows, making for a rocky higher point; however, it passes below it on the right, thus avoiding the cairn built where a pointed rock slab meets the end of a wall running down into Rydale beside the rocks of

The ridge to Heron Pike from Great Rigg.

Erne Crag. Immediately beyond is another small depression and this time the path rises to the cairn on the little outcrop of white quartzite marking Heron Pike. This is the turn-off point for the return to Grasmere and the OS maps show a path from here straight to the foot of Greenhead Gill. Tough luck: there is no sign of one on the ground. It is best to return to the last depression, just north of Heron Pike, where faint traces of a path will be found leading down the steep grass slopes. Even these fade and the best descent is as direct as creaking knee-joints will allow to Alcock Tarn. This is fringed by small crags and favoured as a picnic spot although AW, on what must have been a rare off-day, described it as 'a dreary sheet of water'. A rocky high point near Butter Crag sports a flagpole during the Annual Grasmere Sports each August and it may be of interest to know that the record time, set by Fred Reeves in 1978 and up to now unbeaten, for the ascent *and* descent from Grasmere is 12 mins 21.6 *secs*. The rest of us will do well to take double that time just for the descent.

This is achieved, not down the direct line of the Senior Guides Race, but by the well-used path from the north end of the tarn. This descends down several steep and stony zigzags until it runs beside a wall enclosing conifers, then into the bed of Greenhead Gill. A left turn to a footbridge leads to the end of the metalled drive, where the outward route is rejoined.

Grasmere

4 SEAT SANDAL AND FAIRFIELD FROM GRASMERE

BEST MAP: *OS 1:50 000 Landranger 90 Penrith, Keswick & Ambleside area. At 1:25 000 scale both Outdoor Leisure 7, South Eastern area and 5, North Eastern area are needed.*
APPROXIMATE TIME: *5–6 hours*
TERRAIN: *A long grassy ridge, a stony ascent, good paths and then a trackless descent on grass to pick up good paths on the return.*

ITINERARY	Book & Fell No	Height of ascent	Distance	Cumulative distance	Height above sea level	
		feet	miles	miles	feet	mtrs
GRASMERE					200	61
Seat Sandal	1.17	2200	3.50	3.50	2415	736
Fairfield	1.05	950	1.33	4.83	2863	873
Great Rigg	1.15	140	1.00	5.83	2513	766
Heron Pike	1.25	150	1.50	7.33	2003	612
GRASMERE			2.25	9.58	200	61
Totals of heights and distances		3440	9.58			

This horseshoe round starts from Grasmere to link Seat Sandal, Fairfield, Great Rigg and Heron Pike; it is thus a circuit of the skylines of both Tongue Gill and Greenhead Gill. Seat Sandal is clearly seen from Grasmere, to the east of Dunmail Raise, rising as a gentle grassy slope to a flattened top which ends abruptly where the grinding ice took a large bite from its eastern side, leaving shattered rocks and scree there. It is a good viewpoint and its south ridge is the initial means of gaining height on this round.

Starting from any of Grasmere's car parks, leave the village and walk north along the A591 towards Keswick, passing the Traveller's Rest pub, to where there is a sharp bend at Mill Bridge. Just round the bend a walled lane turns right off the main road, leading up beside a row of modernised cottages and then beside the beck flowing down Tongue Gill. AW showed a route to the south ridge of Seat Sandal which turns off the lane, passes through a gateway on the left beside a barn and then rises through fields, but the farmer got fed up with the traffic so this route is now closed to walkers. Instead, continue to the gate at the end of the lane where open fell is reached.

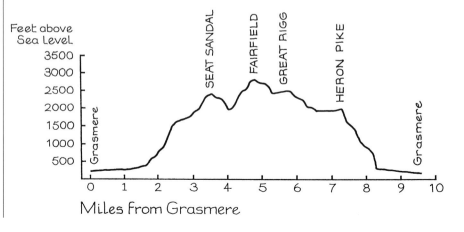

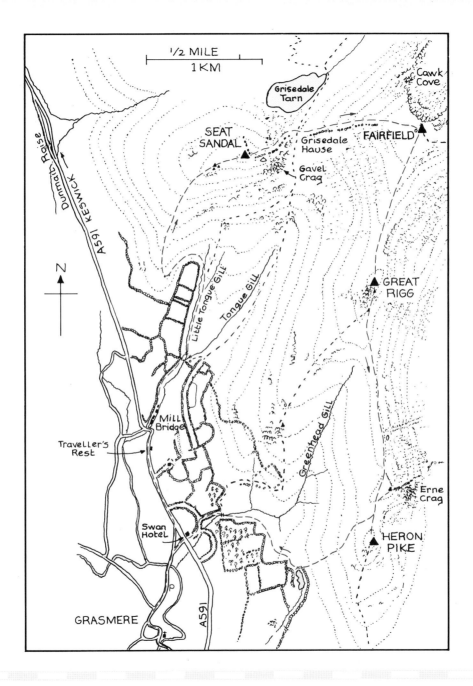

From the gate keep left across a footbridge and then continue up the broad path beside Little Tongue Gill until it crosses the beck at a ford. Now trend away left from the path, cross the other little beck on the left when convenient and follow round the curve of the intake wall leftwards and outside it on a very faint path to reach the south ridge. (Here there is a notice on a post with an arrow-sign advising walkers descending the ridge that there is no access through the enclosed fields lower down.)

The south ridge is not well defined although it sharpens briefly shortly after it is joined, hinting vainly at better things ahead; indeed, the more height is gained the broader it seems to become and it is not really surprising that there isn't much of a path up here. It is with some relief that it levels off at a shoulder on a flat grassy platform. Here there are now three cairns, one larger than the others, so there has been a bit of hanky-panky up here since AW was here. About 300 paces to the north-east and on slightly higher ground is Seat Sandal's main cairn, close to a collapsed wall which crosses the summit and will shortly be useful in showing the line of descent to Grisedale Hause. The best views are definitely those from north-east of the main cairn, overlooking Grisedale Tarn and down Grisedale, with St Sunday Crag and part of Fairfield in the picture.

The route to the next objective, Fairfield, is now also to be seen in depressing clarity – the most direct way being a steep climb up scree, with various zigzagging variations. The descent from Seat Sandal to Grisedale Hause is steep but straightforward, trending left to avoid some small crags. It is interesting to see that one of these, previously anonymous but given the name of Gavel Crag by AW, is now marked and named as such on the OS 1:25 000 maps. The steep climb to Fairfield follows the collapsed remnants of the wall which never, even when young and upright, managed to make it to the top. Thereafter, the direction is well marked by cairns over stones to the broad summit plateau. Here, apart from the lines of cairns ushering walkers along, there is now a circular stone windbreak, superior to the 'tumbledown windbreak of stones, built as a short wall and offering shelter only to persons of imagination' noted by AW. The summit cairn is still there, a short way to the north-east, but there is now also a commodious five-chambered windbreak perched on the edge of the dramatic drop down Cawk Cove to Dovedale, which should greatly please today's persons of imagination. The views from here are worth lingering over, but in anything other than clear weather it is important to ensure that the correct bearing, south, is taken for the next leg, to Great Rigg, as the lines of cairns all look the same in a mist. Even in clear weather walkers go wrong here; I recently met a couple half way down the ridge to St Sunday Crag who thought they were descending directly to Rydal.

Heading south over the stony top, the cairns marking the way soon lead out onto an easier, grassier surface presenting the temptation to gallop along the exhilarating ridge that now shows ahead, curving very slightly round the head of Rydale. Great Rigg is reached with hardly any effort at all apart from the very slight rise to its summit cairn. A

Looking west from the summit of Seat Sandal.

more careful pace is needed for the descent of the broken rocks which lead beyond another, smaller cairn down to the quite large one almost at the base of the rocks; this cairn marks the point where a path forks off to the right, heading for Grasmere via Stone Arthur. Then the pace can hot up again as fast easy walking leads along the slightly undulating ridge to reach a noticeably rocky and higher point (although the path skirts this on its right-hand side) crowned by a cairn. Cairns are common enough but this one is on a pointed rock slab at the top end of a wall running down into Rydale, and just below are the rocks of Erne Crag. The high point itself is not named, which is a pity, because it is more distinctive and identifiable than Heron Pike. This latter summit is slightly lower and just beyond a slight depression ahead and its cairn is located on a little outcrop of quartzite, but if you reach it you have gone too far and you should ignore the path descending steeply down eroded grooves ahead.

From the little depression *before* Heron Pike's summit, therefore, strike down the grassy slopes to the south-west on a faint path. This soon gives out, but as the public foot-path shown on the OS map doesn't exist on the ground at all, it is better than nothing. Little gills begin to develop as you descend but there is no really obvious way until Alcock Tarn comes into view and then faint paths begin to show again, making either for a stile in the wall encircling the tarn at its south end or avoiding the wall entirely by making for the northern end. AW wasn't very kind about Alcock Tarn, calling it 'a dreary sheet of water'.

The main route that AW shows back to Grasmere from Alcock Tarn (and the one on my sketch map) takes a well-used path beside the north end of the tarn and descends steeply down grassy slopes in zigzags to the edge of enclosed conifers. It descends to the bed of Greenhead Gill and then, after crossing the beck (by a little footbridge if needed), turns down a narrow metalled drive to reach a minor road where a left turn quickly leads down to the Swan Hotel on the main A591 opposite the side road into Grasmere village. But on the map for Nab Scar he does show that there are other, and more delight-ful, paths leading from the south, the outlet end of Alcock Tarn back to Grasmere. There is no need to describe them: simply follow your nose downhill on any of the well-used paths, taking in some most attractive views over Grasmere with its island, and when you reach tarmac turn right and right again. You will pass Dove Cottage and the Wordsworth Exhibition and reach Grasmere on the corner of Stocks Lane, by the Prince of Wales Hotel.

Grisedale Tarn, St Sunday Crag and Fairfield from Seat Sandal.

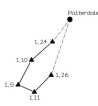

5 THE DEEPDALE HORSESHOE

BEST MAP: *OS 1:25 000 Outdoor Leisure 5, North Eastern area*
APPROXIMATE TIME: *5–6 hours*
TERRAIN: *Almost all on good paths, some stony; a few boggy patches.*

ITINERARY	Book & Fell No	Height of ascent	Distance	Cumulative distance	Height above sea level	
		feet	miles	miles	feet	mtrs
PATTERDALE					500	152
Birks	1.24	1600	1.75	1.75	2040	622
St Sunday Crag	1.10	800	1.25	3.00	2756	841
Fairfield	1.05	750	1.50	4.50	2863	873
Hart Crag	1.11	150	1.00	5.50	2698	822
Hartsop Above How	1.26	150	1.50	7.00	1870	570
PATTERDALE			3.00	10.00	500	152
Totals of heights and distances		3450	10.00			

This is one of the classic horseshoe walks of the Lake District and one of the best, with exhilarating walking and some magnificent mountain scenery, but I would bet that very few walkers have followed the *complete* course, including the ascent of Birks, that is illuminated by the AW ridge-line map. I admit that I had not.

The start is from Patterdale and directly opposite the Patterdale Hotel is a good car park holding about thirty cars (grid ref 396159). Round the back of the hotel is a signed public footpath which leads south through a few birch trees to a kissing-gate. Here it swings south-west and rises to the left of a wall and up to a knoll, passing through a landscape of fine mature beech, ash and oak trees to two gates side by side. Take the left-hand one (footpath sign) which continues ahead to the south-west near to the wall and succeeding fence, curves into a shallow gill to cross Hag Beck on big stones, then

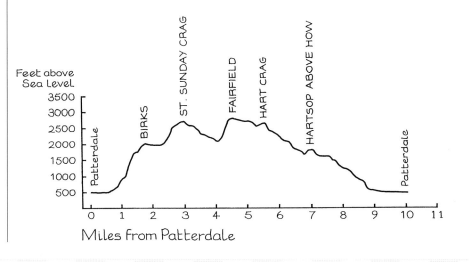

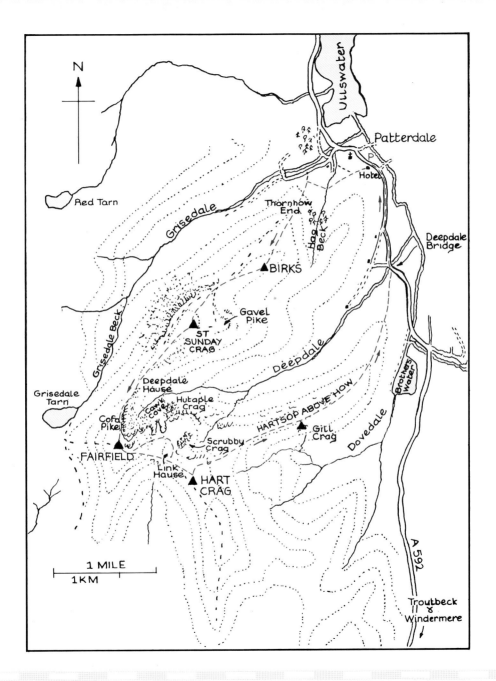

contours across more pastures to reach the spine of the ridge leading up to Thornhow End. That is the approach completed.

Here there is a gate and stile where a path turns downhill to the Patterdale road; instead turn left, beneath some oak trees, and climb steeply uphill – it is steep enough to reduce your gossiping to gasping – on an obvious path up the ridge to a grassy knoll on top of the rock buttress on Thornhow End. From the stile over the intake wall which is immediately ahead, the main path sensibly slants rightwards, and shortly joins a natural groove, but it avoids the spine of the ridge where it is at its sharpest and misses out the summit of Birks completely. Therefore, follow traces of a path up the sharpest and steepest part of the spine but these disappear as height is gained and the way is then over grass and almost trackless. Passing a cairn and a nearby larger heap of stones, which may be all that is left of a beacon, the tiny cairn on the highest grassy point of Birks is soon reached. Beyond rises a large tent-shaped fell, St Sunday Crag, which has Gavel Pike as its left-hand peak.

The main path is rejoined at a hause just ahead, and the route then rises round, over and between the rocks and boulders on the right-hand edge of St Sunday Crag over-looking Grisedale. A cairn marks where a less-used trod slants off left to Gavel Pike but the main path continues up the rocky edge to a stone-studded slope. A line of cairns leads southwards up the slope towards the summit, where there is an untidy heap of stones amidst rocks. It is worth noting that the main path, the one showing most signs of use, does not aim for the summit at all but takes a lower traversing line across the right-hand flank, well above the dramatic line of steep cliffs dropping to Grisedale, and then contours to Deepdale Hause. This route has obviously been developed by fellwalkers exercising a time-honoured practice of dodging the summit.

An easy, stony path continues along the main ridge, descending gently to Deepdale Hause and with a fine prospect ahead of Seat Sandal beyond Grisedale Tarn. To the left, the shaly grass slopes lead down to ice-scoured slabs at the head of Deepdale; to the right is Dollywaggon Pike with the gully-seamed faces of Falcon Crag and Tarn Crag below it; ahead the ridge continues up a steep and rocky slope and looks quite tricky. Closer acquaintance reveals various paths winding between and over the spiky rocks on the ridge, with the most interesting being on the left side. The steeper rock cone of Cofa Pike, near the top of the ridge and sporting a big cairn, is traversed or by-passed easily, allowing a terrific view down Deepdale, especially to the cliffs of Hutaple Crag. Finally a small pinnacle is by-passed on the right and a short rise beyond leads to the summit plateau of Fairfield. The most direct way is up loose and shaly rock on the left edge but it is too loose and exposed for comfort; few walkers venture this way. A little to the right is an easy-angled short gully and an ascent up this leads directly to a cairn with, just beyond it, the five-chambered windbreak on the summit. A third way traverses out to the right at an easy angle and then swings back in a wide loop to the top.

Hutaple Crag seen from Cofa Pike.

In clear weather, there is no problem; in mist, the little gully is the quickest and safest.

    Two lines of cairns lead off the plateau, one to the south for Great Rigg, but the one needed is to the south-east for a hundred paces or so then east, curving round the top of the scree gully leading down to Cawk Cove. The cairned path takes a totally safe line towards Hart Crag, keeping well back from the edge, but a narrower path now skirts it, giving much better views down the north face, including some down the huge gully of Black Tippet at the left (west) side of Hutaple Crag. Regaining the main path nearby, at a point where the ridge is fairly narrow so that steep scree and grass slopes can be seen dropping away to Rydal Head on the right, it soon starts to descend over rocky ground to Link Hause. A well-worn path on stones and gravel climbs up the other side, passing a big cairn on the left which seems to have been built from the stones of a one-time shelter still marked on the OS map. A retrospective view reveals the almost vertical and usually damp rocks of Scrubby Crag frowning over Link Cove and from here also can be seen the line of our continuing ridge descending to Hartsop above How.

Before going that way, however, we need to visit the summit of Hart Crag, which is a little higher, about 100 paces away and has two cairns at each end of a stony but almost level area. Honour is satisfied, but it offers no great views to savour and, leaving the summit, the path can be joined heading north-east. This is over simple stony ground to begin with, but then down the edge of easy-angled but fairly exposed slabs, keeping just to the right of the crest near the bottom, to gain easier angled grass slopes. Here there is a very distinctive and compact little craggy outcrop whose rock is so rough and knobbly it looks as if it came from some volcanic concrete mixer.

The ridge now descends more gently and a path follows the crest across a few peat hags and a depression, then rises slightly to the area called Hartsop above How. Here there is a little cairn on the highest rocky lump, above the rocks of Gill Crag. The name Hartsop above How always seemed an odd one to me, even before I began to study AW's Pictorial Guides and discovered he had felt the same uncertainty. He almost suggests that 'How above Hartsop' would be more accurate, a 'how' being a small hill. Personally, I always preferred to call this the Gill Crag ridge even before I read AW's remarks that 'Most natives of Deepdale … all know Gill Crag which fringes the summit, and this would seem to be a more satisfactory name for the fell.'

This little rocky eminence is only one of several more which the path bypasses on the left. It continues over peat and springy grass and eventually runs alongside a wall which rises from Dovedale and then too strides along the crest of the ridge. There are good views over Dovedale and Brothers Water on this descent and then an easy-angled little rocky staircase is reached. At its foot is a ladder-stile where the wall rises over a little crag on the right. Do *not* cross here but keep on until a transverse wall is reached; this one should be crossed by a ladder-stile and the walk continued, still with the wall running down the spine of the ridge on your right-hand side. The wall remains a useful guide because the path fades and reappears while descending the pleasant sheep pastures that follow, although it does become obvious as it enters a belt of woodland. Descend through this towards the main A592 road and when the path forks, while still in the woodland, the left fork should be taken to reach a ladder-stile over a wall, just about 30 paces right of a barn. A path marked by white arrows on posts now leads across a fine natural meadow to a gate at the main road, near the phone box at Deepdale Bridge. To complete the round, turn left along the road back to Patterdale; fortunately there is a footpath off the tarmac for most of the way, which is just as well when your feet ache.

Brothers Water and Hartsop Dodd from the Hartsop above How ridge.

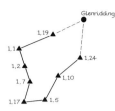

6 THE GRISEDALE SKYLINE

BEST MAP: *OS 1:25000 Outdoor Leisure 5, North Eastern area.*
APPROXIMATE TIME: *8 hours*
TERRAIN: *An untracked scramble-walk to start, then good paths on rock and over mixed ground.*

ITINERARY	Book & Fell No	Height of ascent	Distance	Cumulative distance	Height above sea level	
		feet	miles	miles	feet	mtrs
GLENRIDDING					600	183
Birkhouse Moor	1.19	1900	1.50	1.50	2350	718
Helvellyn	1.01	800	2.00	3.50	3118	949
Nethermost Pike	1.02	80	0.75	4.25	2920	891
Dollywaggon Pike	1.07	120	1.00	5.25	2810	858
Seat Sandal	1.17	600	1.25	6.50	2415	736
Fairfield	1.05	950	1.33	7.83	2863	873
St Sunday Crag	1.10	610	1.50	9.33	2756	841
Birks	1.24	50	1.25	10.58	2040	622
GLENRIDDING			2.00	12.58	600	183
Totals of heights and distances		5110	12.58			

Including Striding Edge, which is almost certainly the most popular ridge in the whole of the eastern fells, this complete circuit is also one of the longest and best for mountain scenery. In addition, the ridge-line map based on AW's routes reveals an interesting variation on the rather dull plod beside Mires Beck, which is the standard route to Helvellyn from Glenridding. This variation is a scramble-walk, directly up the north-east ridge of Birkhouse Moor, and I recommend it.

There is a large and convenient car park in Glenridding (grid ref 385169) which is left by a little snicket at its west end, signed 'Helvellyn via Greenside', to reach Greenside Road. A left turn up the hill between terraced cottages, many built originally for miners working in the nearby lead-mines and slate quarries, leads to a fork in the road; a good view of Birkhouse Moor's north-east ridge is revealed directly ahead. Take the left fork and go downhill to cross Rattlebeck Bridge. A track now rises past the caravan site in the valley bottom and up the walled lane beyond. Ignore the path (at the first wall)

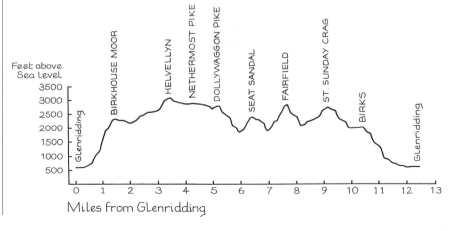

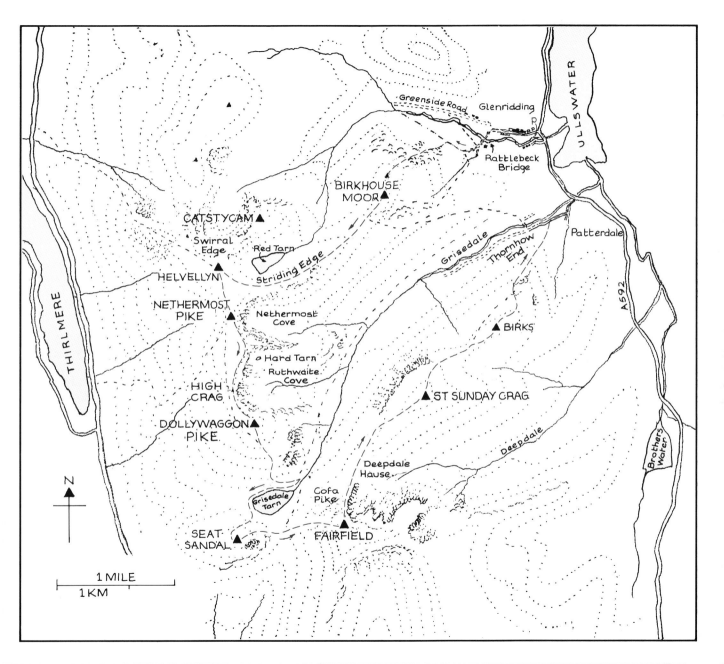

off to the right and signed for Greenside Mines; instead, continue uphill, bearing right at a little coppice (signs for Helvellyn) to a second transverse wall. Here there is a gate and ladder-stile and at this point the popular Mires Beck track for Helvellyn goes left. Aged or infirm walkers may prefer this dull route, especially in high summer when the bracken may be tall, but walkers fancying a bit of excitement will, however, turn right here and follow a grassy path just uphill of the wall. This soon reaches the obvious blunt end of the north-east ridge of Birkhouse Moor. Turn up a tongue of grass between bracken, shortly crossing the line of the old water-race, to pick a way up grassy ledges and between junipers through the scattered rock outcrops. There is no path but the way up is all very obvious, the ridge essentially rising in two steps, with easier sections between. The upper step is steeper and more interesting (which means a bit harder!), then a long slope of easy-angled grass completes the ascent. As AW says, this 'is the best way up, with a beautiful view in retrospect' offering 'a mild adventure' and a 'test in route-finding amongst low crags'. A large cairn is reached on what is the logical top of Birkhouse Moor, but about a quarter-mile further on a section of wall can be seen on a rounded hump of land, and here there is another cairn marking the official summit. On the way you will pick up a laid path (stones in the bog) and join the re-directed Mires Beck route which is marked by white-topped posts.

Helvellyn is now in view and a walk beside the wall towards it soon reaches the point where the other main path rising from Patterdale crosses it by a ladder-stile. This place, marked on the OS maps as 'Hole-in-the-Wall' is incidentally, the last bit of shelter before Striding Edge and if extra clothing needs to be put on, now is the time to do it.

The path is now unmistakable, traversing fairly rough and stony ground in a rising line on the right-hand side of the ridge which affords a little shelter from southerly winds, climbing gradually to reach High Spying How. From here Striding Edge stretches ahead, with a slight descent to reach it, the most interesting path sticking faithfully to the largely flat tops of the rock pinnacles along the crest although more cautious walkers have created separate ones on either side. Just after beginning Striding Edge, a little cross may be spotted on a rock slab overlooking Nethermost Cove on the left; this is the Dixon Memorial, commemorating the death of a chap who was following the hounds of the Patterdale Hunt in 1858 and fell off the ridge. It may give some walkers a little frisson of extra excitement.

But except in high wind or under ice and snow, when the traverse can be an expedition, there are no difficulties that a reasonably agile walker cannot deal with, including the short wide groove where there is a descent of about 20ft at the end of the level section. An easier variation by-passes even this on the left. Ahead, after crossing or by-passing one more little rock upthrust, a fairly steep slope of shale and loose rock leads towards Helvellyn's summit plateau, the most-used path trending rightwards and emerging next to the Gough Memorial. This is a tablet of stone mounted in a rock cairn

Approaching Striding Edge from Birkhouse Moor.

and telling the story, mostly in Wordsworth's verse, of how Charles Gough's dog apparently stayed with his corpse (after he too had fallen from the rocks in 1805) for three months before the body was discovered. Nowadays it is virtually certain that Striding Edge is visited every day of the year.

A right turn on reaching the plateau leads to the four-chambered windbreak that has acted as lunching place for countless walkers, and inevitably a scrap-scrounging place for my two little dogs. The highest point is just behind it on some insignificant rocks and the summit trig found just to the north-west. The views from the plateau, down to

Striding Edge seen from the upper slopes of Nethermost Cove.

Striding Edge forming one arm encircling Red Tarn and Swirral Edge the other, as well as down and beyond Nethermost Cove to St Sunday Crag, Fairfield and the far eastern fells can be superb; I am sure I have been here at least forty times and have never failed to take some photographs.

A well-worn path, almost a motorway, leads south from Helvellyn, with a ludicrous number of cairns piled along the route, but ignore it and follow round the rim of Nethermost Cove where several broken rock buttresses thrust into impressive depths, falling to Grisedale far below. There are two cairns on Nethermost Pike, the biggest amongst spiky rocks, the smaller on the best viewpoint. A very short descent down grass from Nethermost Pike leads to the rocks at the top of a much-neglected ridge which gives a good ascent or descent to Grisedale and which separates Nethermost Cove from Ruthwaite Cove (on the right). A tiny pool, Hard Tarn, can be spotted on a little rock ledge just down the slope in Ruthwaite Cove. Continuing around the rim, a slight descent follows and then a rise to a cairn on the grassy top of High Crag, where another fractured rock buttress thrusts into Ruthwaite Cove; then a further descent and climb leads to Dollywaggon Pike. Here, another subsidiary ridge, The Tongue, thrusts down towards Grisedale, also giving a good but disregarded descent or ascent. St Sunday Crag's gully-seamed north-west face is well seen from here.

Leaving the summit of Dollywaggon Pike down a grassy incline to the south, the prospect ahead is rather daunting, especially when your knee-joints are getting a bit knackered, as mine are. Reaching an iron fence-post on a corner where the 'motorway' is joined as it turns downhill, Grisedale Tarn can be seen glinting in a bowl at the head of Grisedale. This is dominated by Fairfield's long and shaly north-west-facing slopes and is also overlooked by Seat Sandal's rough north-east face. The walk continues over Seat Sandal, but the long descent down the south slope of Dollywaggon Pike has to be faced first. This is not a pleasurable descent, but it is even worse for the walkers who persist in toiling up its eroded course: it really needs channelling into a series of zigzags. When the bottom of the slope is reached, a slight diversion to the Brothers Parting Stone, hardly ever visited by passing walkers, may be of interest and give a good excuse for a breather before the next stage.

The memorial is found just to the right of the main path down Grisedale, a short way below the outlet from Grisedale Tarn. It is well marked by an iron post cemented into the top of the stone, which is like a small crag facing down Grisedale; there is a plaque on top of the post which says 'The Brothers Parting Wordsworth'. Below the plaque, the almost vertical face of rock has been smoothed and about eight lines of verse chiselled into it. I have only been able to distinguish the first three words, 'Here did west …' but the place marks the spot where William Wordsworth said goodbye to his sailor brother who was leaving to join his ship. William waved and watched him disappear down Grisedale, but never saw him again since the boat foundered and he was drowned.

Returning to Grisedale Tarn and contouring round its north shore, AW purists will now tackle the rough grass, stony ground and concealed boulders that make up Seat Sandal's north ridge. Needless to say there is little sign of a path at present, although given time there surely will be one. The slope, tracing the line of a collapsed wall, leads with much effort directly to the main cairn on the summit from where there is a grand view down Grisedale.

Walkers of less stern resolution will go up to the top of Seat Sandal and down again by the same well-marked route that the purists use for their descent, namely down beside the collapsed wall that leads to Grisedale Hause. From here the route to Fairfield is inexorably uphill again, up a steep shaly slope, zigzagging where possible but with no real difficulty in ascent. As the angle eases, a line of cairns leads onto the fell's summit plateau where there is a circular windbreak, the summit cairn close to it and a multi-chambered windbreak built on the edge of the tremendous drop to Deepdale far below.

Curving off to the north, a shaly slope can be seen descending to a little subsidiary peak, Cofa Pike. This is now the way to go, an exhilarating descent down a shallow gully in the shaly slope, over the top of Cofa Pike and then down the easy rock grooves and ledges that follow to reach the hause. A steady ascent, with marvellous views now across the trench of Grisedale to Helvellyn's east-facing combes and to Dollywaggon Pike, now leads to the cairn amidst the summit rocks of St Sunday Crag, which will probably be reached with some relief as it concludes the last major ascent of the day.

A descent down stone-studded slopes to the north, following a line of cairns, leads to the top of a ridge of rocks and boulders that continues more sharply downhill to a wide grassy hause. From here the main path now slants across the fellside below Birks, shortly joining a natural groove which could be followed unerringly downhill. Our ridge-line, however, goes over the summit of Birks, an undistinguished place apart from being a Wainwright top, but then continues down grass slopes to reach the sharpening north ridge which leads, with much more pleasure despite having only traces of a path, to join the main track at a ladder-stile over the wall at Thornhow End. The descent continues down the grassy ridge that follows, via a gate and ladder-stile, to a last gate onto a minor road. A right turn downhill here leads rapidly to the main A592, and a turn left along this, making use of a path just off the road on the left-hand side, soon leads back to the car park at Glenridding. A tough day; a grand day.

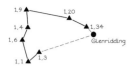

7 THE GLENRIDDING HORIZON

BEST MAP: *OS 1:25 000 Outdoor Leisure 5, North Eastern area*
APPROXIMATE TIME: *7½ hours*
TERRAIN: *Some ill-defined or non-existent grassy paths, particularly on the first half of the walk, joining firm and well-defined ones for the return.*

ITINERARY	Book & Fell No	Height of ascent	Distance	Cumulative distance	Height above sea level	
		feet	miles	miles	feet	mtrs
GLENRIDDING					600	183
Glenridding Dodd	1.34	1000	1.00	1.00	1425	442
Sheffield Pike	1.20	880	1.00	2.00	2232	675
Stybarrow Dodd	1.09	1000	2.00	4.00	2770	845
Raise	1.04	470	1.00	5.00	2889	883
White Side	1.06	200	0.75	5.75	2832	863
Helvellyn	1.01	600	1.50	7.25	3118	949
Catstycam	1.03	320	1.00	8.25	2917	890
GLENRIDDING			4.00	12.25	600	183
Totals of heights and distances		4470	12.25			

This is an interesting but rather strenuous circuit and the northern arm of it has been little-visited. It would not be advisable to set out in misty conditions or bad weather.

The first objective is the unjustly neglected top of Glenridding Dodd and there is a large convenient car park in Glenridding below its steep south slope and beside Glenridding Beck (grid ref 386169). From here, turn up the village street to where it forks just beyond the houses. Take the right fork, signed 'Bridleway Greenside Mine Keppel Cove' and keep on uphill to reach a cattle-grid immediately before some cottages. Here turn right uphill beside a shallow dry gill running down from the hause between Sheffield Pike (ahead on the left) and Glenridding Dodd (on the right). The start is unclear but then a footpath sign (hidden by summer bracken) indicates a better path traversing rightwards to a good viewpoint over Ullswater. The steep rise back left to the hause above gives a good excuse to pause, stop or even sit down to admire views up Glenridding Beck.

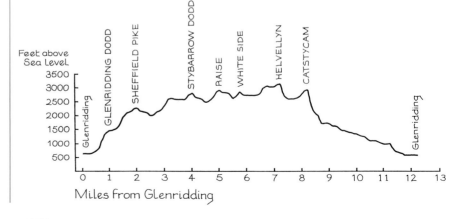

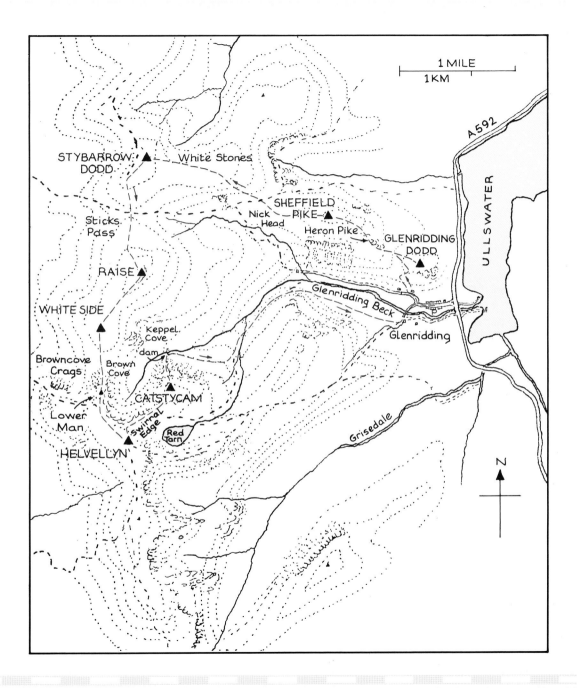

STYBARROW
DODD

White Stones

SHEFFIELD
PIKE

Nick
Head

Sticks
Pass

Heron Pike

GLENRIDDING
DODD

RAISE

ULLSWATER

A592

WHITE SIDE

Keppel
Cove

Glenridding Beck

Browncove
Crags

dam

Brown
Cove

Glenridding

CATSTYCAM

Lower
Man

Swirral
Edge

Red
Tarn

HELVELLYN

Grisedale

1 MILE
1 KM

N

51

The ridge rising to Heron Pike from Glenridding Dodd.

At the wall on the hause, turn right and zigzag up a grassy shoulder, to reach a cairn piled on the highest point of rock on Glenridding Dodd. The larch trees still do not extend to the top of the fell on the north side, as AW noted, and it is bilberry rather than heather which now clothes the summit.

Herons nested, or at least perched, on almost as many Lakeland pikes and crags as ravens, and in sight now is another Heron Pike. This one has a well-defined south-east ridge and the prospect of continuing up it towards the as yet unseen Sheffield Pike will raise a little glow of pleasant anticipation. So return to the hause and follow a vague path first near the wall and then through a wide gap in it. A few cairns mark a route over bilberry, heather and some stretches of rocky ground, to Heron Pike, at the top of the crags overlooking Ullswater. Here is a flat blade of iron, about 2ft 6ins high set upright into a stone, rather like Excalibur, with M 1912 engraved on one side and H 1912 on the other. AW tells us that this marked the boundary between the Howard estate of Greystoke and the Marshall estate of Patterdale. A peaty depression lies ahead, with several pools lurking in it, then an ill-defined rising walk across grass and heather moorland to the north-east, making for the nearest of two cairns which become visible ahead on Sheffield Pike. Somewhere here AW shows a small shelter (described as 'quite useless') which I did not find, but a little further west is a much bigger cairn, on the summit, with a sharp spike of rock stuck into it and the letters M and H carved on

opposite sides. There is an equally useless stone shelter just below this top also; I was jabbed in the back by a sharp stone in every position I chose.

Heading west off Sheffield Pike, a few more soggy-edged tarns are passed on the way to the depression of Nick Head, the view ahead being dominated by a line of level grey spoil, the residue of old mining and smelting operations. Here, about 100 yards from the gap, is a second iron boundary post, engraved like the first. Beyond it, to the north-west, can be seen a faint trod rising up a long grass slope on the broad back of the ridge rising to White Stones and, eventually, Stybarrow Dodd. This trod shortly cuts across another

Glenridding Dodd and Ullswater seen from Heron Pike.

Looking north to Ullswater from Heron Pike: note the iron boundary post.

path, then continues uphill to skirt an old quarried area of substantial size. The faint path continues up the broad back of the ridge to the north-west, with the grass getting shorter as height is gained. Eventually a few rocks appear, with a single cairn, then a second. A third is about 150 paces to the north-west amongst more rocks. This is White Stones.

Beyond, easy grass slopes curve down and then rise to a higher plateau ahead. On the left, across Sticks Gill, can be seen the two huts and pylons used for the ski-tow area on the north-east slope of Raise; you have to be tough to cart your skis on your back up here. A faint path leads forward from White Stones towards an isolated little group of boulders, one of which is shaped like a boundary stone, on an indefinite hause, but this path then tends left, contouring towards Sticks Pass. This is no use, as Stybarrow Dodd is directly ahead, its smooth, rounded grass slopes interrupted by only one rock outcrop at the head of a small gill. So climb the unmarked grass slopes, heading west and then curving north, towards the highest land, reaching the remnants of a wall at the top of the little rocky outcrop. The collapsed wall ends nearly at the top of the fell, some of its stones forming an almost circular windbreak and being easily the biggest man-made structure on the summit area. About 80 paces to the south-west, with hardly another rock in sight, is a little cairn of mostly quartzite stones with an unusual blade of slate stuck in it; this is the summit of Stybarrow Dodd and is the one AW identified, with many entertaining proofs and calculations, as the true one.

The main path along the ridge of the Dodds curves just below its top here, a few paces down the slight slope to the west, and this should now be joined as it leads out along a grassy promontory to another obvious cairn a short quarter-mile to the south-west, and a second smaller cairn just beyond. A clear path descends the easy-angled slopes to the broad wet hause of Sticks Pass and a stony track gives an uphill trudge marked by cairns to the summit of Raise – unusual, as AW noted, in that it is the only summit in the Helvellyn range to be 'adorned with a crown of rough rocks', instead of the monotonous grass, and thus deserving 'a special cheer'. A line of cairns and an obvious path lead off to the south-west, but I didn't notice the iron estate-boundary post mentioned by AW, and pedestrian traffic in the forty years since he wrote this guide has certainly made some paths.

On the descent from Raise towards White Side (marked on the OS 1:25 000 map as Whiteside Bank), the prospect is much more exciting, with the fine cone of Catstycam rising strongly beyond Keppel Cove, its north-west ridge forming its left-hand skyline. The descent from Raise is to a wide col, then an easy-angled ascent on an obvious path leads to the top of White Side where there is little other than more grass and a large untidy cairn. A further short descent leads to a long, stony ridge which, I know from experience, can be very exposed in a wind. From here, there are views down both sides, to Brown Cove on the left-hand side of the ridge and, rather oddly, to Brown Cove Crags on the right-hand side of the same ridge. This culminates at Helvellyn Lower Man, with a little cairn in an expanse of flat stones. A backward glance will reveal all the ground covered so far except Stybarrow Dodd.

A slight descent leads towards the rim of Brown Cove and a broad path coming from Thirlmere via Helvellyn Gill (which is now the most popular route up the west side of Helvellyn) is joined and leads onto the summit plateau of Helvellyn. On the final short rise, Swirral Edge can be seen curving down and then rising to Catstycam, the last top on the circuit. The top of Swirral Edge is marked by a cairn about 100 paces to the north-west of Helvellyn's summit trig point; the four-sided windbreak is a similar distance and at a slightly lower level in the opposite direction. I am glad to say that AW's strictures about decaying heaps of litter here are no longer deserved; clearly walkers are much better behaved now than they were in the fifties.

Swirral Edge is a mass of rock spikes and tumbled blocks and the early part of the descent is down a series of rock grooves, where care is needed in poor conditions, but then paths form on each side and also along the crest; the crest, of course, gives the most sporting route and at its end the walker is just padding along on the top of flat slabs. Avoid turning down the path striking off to the right, heading for the outlet from Red Tarn below; instead, stay on the now rising path along the crest to the pointed circular summit of Catstycam.

AW mentions that the quickest and easiest descent to Glenridding is down the east shoulder, which now has a path down it, but he also suggests, as one of the two *ascent* routes, that 'walkers with red blood in their veins should give their attention to the north-west ridge'. Despite its formidable appearance (already seen from White Side), he describes it as 'actually an easy uphill walk'. As a descent, it is described also as 'easy but too steep for comfort' reflecting the almost universal experience that, as you get older, it is harder on the legs going down than up. Just because of the implied challenge, but *not* in bad weather, I suggest this is the way to go now. In fact, there is now a reasonable path down but it snakes down some fairly loose scree and care is needed on rocks near the bottom where the ridge steepens a little. There is a bit more loose scree at the end.

Completion of the descent leads to the breached dam, bristling with rusted metal tie-rods, which once held Keppelcove Tarn; the fractured concrete looks like grey corn-flakes. From here, contouring below the north face of Catstycam, the line of an old aqueduct can be followed until it connects with the well-used path to Glenridding from Red Tarn, shortly crossing Redtarn Beck by a footbridge. A little further on is a second footbridge and then the remains of a wall, with big concrete blocks at the bottom and an iron cog-wheel lying in the stream below; apparently the remains of an old pipeline. A wide and well-used path now leads down the valley, keeping on the south (right) bank of the beck on a good path, embanked in places and probably the course of the old leat. When a grassy path slants off it to the left, follow this, running just outside the intake wall; it joins the Mires Beck path at a gate and ladder-stile. A last descent down fields, with Sheffield Pike facing across the valley, leads past the caravan and camp site by Rattlebeck Bridge and a right turn leads back down to the car park.

Catstycam, with a profile of the north-west ridge, from Lower Man.

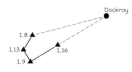

8 THE NORTHERN DEEPDALE CIRCUIT

BEST MAP: *OS 1:25 000 Outdoor Leisure 5, North Eastern area*
APPROXIMATE TIME: *5½–6 hours*
TERRAIN: *Mostly pathless but easy-on-the-feet walking over rolling grassy ground, which can occasionally be very wet.*

ITINERARY	Book & Fell No	Height of ascent	Distance	Cumulative distance	Height above sea level	
		feet	miles	miles	feet	mtrs
DOCKRAY					950	290
Great Dodd	1.08	2000	4.75	4.75	2807	856
Watson's Dodd	1.13	0	0.75	5.50	2584	789
Stybarrow Dodd	1.09	200	0.67	6.17	2770	845
Hart Side	1.16	300	1.50	7.67	2481	756
DOCKRAY			4.00	11.67	950	290
Totals of heights and distances		2500	11.67			

Apart from the well-known Deepdale draining waters from Fairfield to Ullswater, there is another Deepdale in the eastern Lakeland fells, the source of Aira Beck and the well-known Aira Force. The high fells that encircle it are Great Dodd, Watson's Dodd, Stybarrow Dodd and Hart Side; they form a fellwalker's circuit that is most untypical of Lakeland but still has much of interest and the return on the high land above Ullswater gives some good views. I admit that I put off doing this round for a long time because I already knew some of the ground and I didn't fancy it again, but in the event, despite poor weather, I had a thoroughly enjoyable day.

AW started his ascent from Dockray, but every little spot which you might choose to leave your car has a notice put up to discourage exactly that. So unless you are being dropped off, it is better to go to High Row just a mile to the north-west of Dockray. On a 90° bend at the end of the old coach road to Threlkeld (grid ref 381219), there is

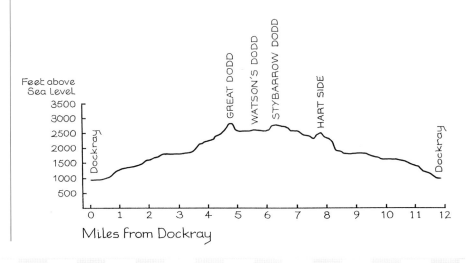

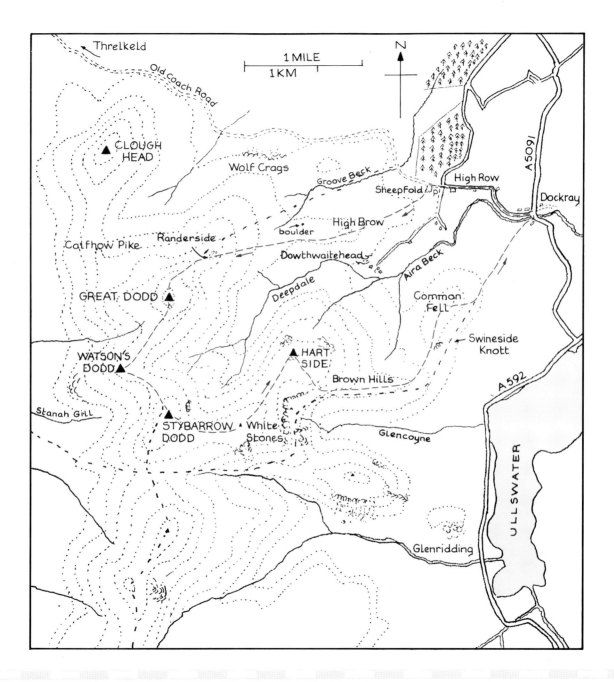

AW's boulder on High Brow, looking towards Randerside and Great Dodd.

a sheepfold and a National Trust sign for 'Matterdale Common'; here a dozen cars can park although para-gliders fly from Wolf Crags above the old coach road and use the same parking place.

The ridge line mentioned by AW leads from High Row to an eminence, not a very big eminence, named High Brow and then to Randerside, avoiding the 'abominably marshy' path up Groove Beck. To follow it, go through the gate next to the sheepfold and onto the old coach road but leave it almost immediately and go WSW on a grassy track, shortly leaving that (to keep true to the bearing) and head for an obvious grassy hill ahead, keeping the wall enclosing the hamlet of Dowthwaitehead well on the left. The hill is High Brow, with a grassy top and a small cairn. From here the lonely headwaters of Deepdale are displayed, the rest of the circuit is in view and you too will be wondering why you are here at all. Take heart; it improves, but not yet.

Due west is a little outcrop of crags on Randerside, with the rounded bulk of Great Dodd behind it and to the left. The way there involves a slight descent across a broad grassy top decorated, if that's the word, with a few peat hags and stagnant pools, passing a group of four or five boulders on the left of the line of march, which would be un-worthy of notice but for their rarity in these acres of grass. AW has given fame on his map to a single boulder, just to the right and a little further on, so I went to investigate;

in fact, it is four big boulders and two tiny ones but they are all so close together that they look like one.

The trudge to Randerside is like any other trudge except that there is no path so it is that much harder. On arrival, the rocks are found to be round the edges of a small rectangular and mostly grassy platform. There are two cairns; the smaller looks just a whisker higher, hardly worth the effort of building it. Clough Head is in sight to the north-west, as is the strange little rock outcrop of Calfhow Pike, seen peeping round the shoulder of Great Dodd, whose long grassy slopes are now directly ahead.

The footpath from Groove Beck avoids the top of Randerside by a few paces but you may as well join it as it runs obviously up a groove towards what seems, from below, to be the top of Great Dodd. Near the actual top, however, it tends noticeably to the right and, while still rising, comes to an abrupt end at a cairn. When I arrived, by now in low cloud and rain – weather conditions which seemed somehow appropriate – this caused me a certain amount of consternation since it was obviously not the top. On the basis of 'If in doubt, go uppards' I turned upslope, soon spotted another cairn and then a large one, the summit.

Since AW's visit, when this point was apparently marked only by a 'naked stone thrusting through the turf', the cairn-builders have been at work. However, about two hundred yards away to the south-east and at a slightly lower level, the hollowed-out stone windbreak is still there and provides better views than the summit.

From the windbreak, a grassy path descends gently to the south-west, being joined at its lowest point by another coming from Calfhow Pike, this path being developed by walkers doing the common trick of dodging the summit, in this case of Great Dodd. Just beyond this point, three grassy paths develop, two of them being fairly close together and curving round the head of Browndale Beck on the left, making for the peaty slope rising towards Stybarrow Dodd (doing it again, this time dodging Watson's Dodd). The path you want trends right and, after passing a couple of tiny tarns on the left, continues along this almost level plateau to reach the small summit cairn on Watson's Dodd. Here you are out on a grassy promontory, with steep slopes sweeping down to Stanah Gill and Thirlmere and you can feel superior to the walkers who have avoided it.

An obvious grassy path leads over to join the other two, now merged, climbing the slope to Stybarrow Dodd, but again it curves just below the highest point of the fell and continues for a further quarter-mile out to another promontory, where there is another cairn and a view down to Sticks Pass. But Stybarrow Dodd's summit must be visited or you will lose the line of the walk, so leave the path and turn up the very short slope to the small summit cairn of mostly quartzite stones, in the middle of which is a single spike of blue slate. Nearby, to the north-east, is a little circular stone windbreak built from the stones of a collapsed wall which runs down the slope to the east.

The next stretch is pathless and you cannot, even in good visibility, immediately see the next objective, so take a bearing south-east and head down grass slopes, curving slightly round the headwaters of Aira Beck to reach a broad hause. Here there is a little group of stones, one of which may be a boundary stone, and from this point a faint path rises towards the small groups of rocks on White Stones which the OS seem to have re-named since AW drew his map when he identified the area as Green Side. There are three cairns in line here on this very broad ridge, the largest being the first one reached.

Hart Side can now be seen; the line of the ridge continues towards it just east of north and a faint track on grass heads in that direction, passing a shallow pool on the depression after which there is a gentle rise to the top. Here there is a curious trench, about a hundred yards long, the excavated stones being cast up on either side. These must be those 'evidences that men laboured on these lonely heights' mentioned by AW. Again there are three cairns, this time within fifty paces of each other, the most northerly looking out over Deepdale to the unmistakable shape of Great Mell Fell which AW aptly described as an 'inverted pudding-basin'.

The paths now disappear completely as you swing south-east down to a slight depression, over the rise beyond and down long grass slopes above the north side of the very steep ground of Glencoyne Head. The objective is a point on the collapsed wall running over the fell from Deepdale just before it descends precipitously to Glencoyne. When crossed, you step onto the Brown Hills ridge. (The path shown on the OS map going left to Dowthwaitehead, which might tempt you to desert the route, cannot be seen on the ground and has apparently disappeared in marshy land.)

A faint path seems to run over the reddish-brown grass along the ridge top, keeping above the line of the main path lower down the slope, but eventually your doubts turn to certainty: there is no path. It is a good chance to demonstrate strength of character and stay on the rougher ground to reach Swineside Knott. The reward is a good view along Ullswater. Even more strength (and well-greased boots) is needed to remain on the ridge over tussocky, wiry grass and bog which have to be traversed to reach the little cairn on Common Fell, but it yields a good view back up Deepdale. Just below the top is a solitary boulder on a rock plinth, then more grass slopes swoop down towards Dockray. It is impossible, and unnecessary, now to avoid joining the main path but its course is a little confused by tractor tracks and it is abominably wet. It leads just to the right of a little beck directly to the village, then a short walled lane, with a telephone box at its end, leads to a junction with the main A5091. A left turn brings another junction and you may well be pleased to see the Royal Hotel on the corner, because the walk back to High Row from here is almost all uphill. Hard luck.

Stybarrow Dodd seen from White Stones.

ITINERARY	Book & Fell No	Height of ascent	Distance	Cumulative distance	Height above sea level	
		feet	miles	miles	feet	mtrs
Wanthwaite					450	137
Clough Head	1.18	1900	2.00	2.00	2381	726
Great Dodd	1.08	720	2.00	4.00	2807	856
Watson's Dodd	1.13	0	0.75	4.75	2584	789
Stybarrow Dodd	1.09	200	0.67	5.42	2770	845
Raise	1.04	470	1.00	6.42	2889	883
White Side	1.06	200	0.75	7.17	2832	863
Helvellyn	1.01	600	1.50	8.67	3118	949
Nethermost Pike	1.02	80	0.75	9.42	2920	891
Dollywaggon Pike	1.07	120	1.00	10.42	2810	858
Seat Sandal	1.17	600	1.25	11.67	2415	736
Fairfield	1.05	950	1.33	13.00	2863	873
Great Rigg	1.15	140	1.00	14.00	2513	766
Heron Pike	1.25	150	1.50	15.50	2003	612
Nab Scar	1.33	0	0.67	16.17	1450	442
Rydal			1.00	17.17	250	76
Ambleside			1.50	18.67	250	76
Totals of heights and distances		6130	18.67			

9 THE BACKBONE OF THE EASTERN FELLS (a traverse)

BEST MAP: *OS 1:50 000 Landranger 90 Penrith, Keswick & Ambleside area, but apart from the finish of the walk, it will all be found on OS 1:25 000 Outdoor Leisure 5, North Eastern area*
APPROXIMATE TIME: *9–10 hours*
TERRAIN: *An initial stiff climb on scree and grass, then easy high-level walking on good paths until stonier ground on the highest tops.*

Walked in a north to south direction, with the height gained quickly and the easiest walking rattled off in the morning, this fine traverse has a gradual buildup to its highest and most dramatic fells rather than a long decline from them. In addition, the final descent to Ambleside is on well-used paths on which surely nobody could get lost. The northern part of the walk is generally known as the Dodds Ridge; it could in all fairness be called the Dodger's Ridge for the main path along it carefully avoids every summit, which is worth remembering in mist. As this walk is a traverse, it will obviously be necessary to be dropped off on the B5322 running through St John's in the Vale, either at the approach to the disused Bramcrag Quarry (grid ref 319219) for the start by way of Fisher's Wife's Rake; or, for the other approach described from near Wanthwaite, just under ¾ mile further north along the road from the quarry where there is a sign 'Matterdale unsuitable for motors' (grid ref 316231).

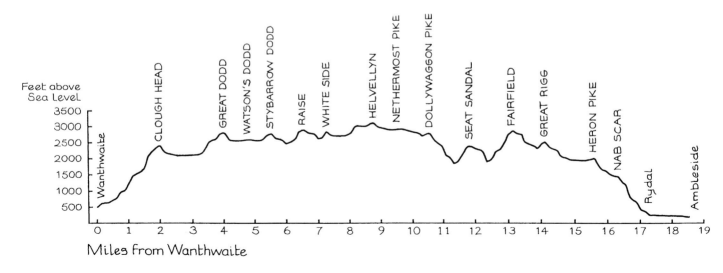

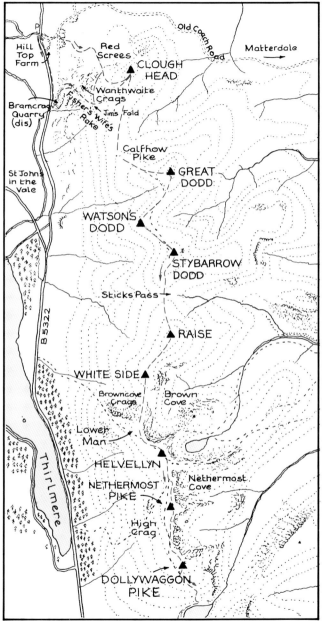

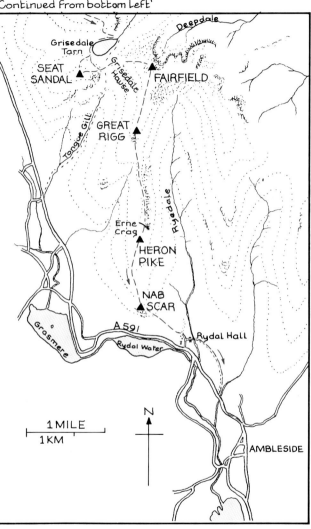

'Continued top right'

'Continued from bottom left'

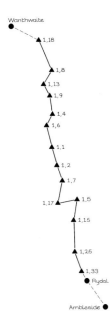

Clough Head, overlooking St John's in the Vale, is the first top, a grassy summit guarded by a wall of crags with just one breach. This is Fisher's Wife's Rake and, to use one of AW's own phrases, any walkers with red blood in their veins will want to use it.

For the Rake, AW's approach is out of date as a stile off the road (B5322) no longer exists and there is an extra fence. Instead, walk up the approach road into the disused Bramcrag Quarry. This swings back sharp left, then continue along it past three shale roads turning into the quarry to a fourth, which is grassy, just in front of a small concrete shed. Turn right here to find a gate onto open fell where the intake wall meets a fence, next to a solitary pine tree. The breach of Fisher's Wife's Rake is then seen directly above and slightly left. A grass tongue leads up it to the left end of a belt of light-coloured crags, then curves back right above them, emerging onto grassy fell above the fiercely steep ravine of Sandbed Gill. A sharp turn back north-east from the sheepfold (Jim's Fold) now leads up grass slopes (not much sign of a path, surprise, surprise) to Clough Head.

Omitting the longest and dreariest approach, up the grassy north-east ridge of Clough Head from Hause Well, the other two approaches start about ¾ mile further north along the road from Bramcrag Quarry. The sign 'Matterdale unsuitable for motors' points off the B5322 along a track, the old coach road to the north of Clough Head. It leads past Hill Top Farm, keeping left when it forks. As it turns north and the wall on the right ends, watch for a step-stile over the wire fence on the right, near three ash trees backed by a spoil tip. A path climbs steeply to cross the level terrace of the old mineral line (finger-post at the crossing) and continues up the left edge of a deep quarry to another step-stile over a wire fence. Just beyond is a ladder-stile over the intake wall onto open fell. From here a path climbs a groove to the south-east, zigzagging to climb in a slanting line through the steeper ground of Red Screes, reaching a grassy shoulder to the south-west of Clough Head. A turn to the ENE up grassy slopes then leads to the trig point and windbreak on the summit.

The alternative finish to this approach is AW's more 'sporting' route. This leaves the path below the last part of the ascent up Red Screes and traverses right towards and then behind a prominent rock spike, continuing an exhilarating traverse above Wanthwaite Crags to reach Jim's Fold. (This is not for those who get into a dither looking down from heights.) Get any little stones out of your boots here and then flog up grass slopes to the north-east to Clough Head. It is a fine viewpoint for Blencathra and as good as any other for Great Dodd, the next objective.

That is all the hard work well and truly over for a long way as what now follows is essentially an undulating scenic walk for several miles along a rolling grassy ridge. The rock outcrop of Calfhow Pike, slightly downhill to the south, is the only solid object in acres of rippling grass, then the path climbs a gradual slope to a cairn on Little Dodd. Cheats dodge Great Dodd by following the path cutting across Millgill Head but true top-baggers swing left up the slope to the small cairn on its rounded grass top and take

Blencathra seen from Wanthwaite Crags: note fox prints.

a breather in the stone windbreak in the rocks about 200 yards to the south-east. An obvious path now descends gradually south-west to an almost level ridge, but do keep to the right-hand of the three paths that soon appear in order to reach the cairn out on the promontory of Watson's Dodd. A switch to the south-east picks up the main path again on the peaty slope towards Stybarrow Dodd but, yet again, you will have to veer left to the actual summit cairn, made mostly of quartzite stones. There is a circular wind-break close by at the end of a collapsed wall running down the slope to the east.

Returning to the main path, this heads south-west now to a cairn at the top of the slope above Sticks Pass, and the way is obvious from there to Raise, although the ground underfoot changes from squelchy bog to peaty grough to sharp stones on the ascent. The summit cairn is found within grey rock outcrops, the first real rock since Calfhow Pike, but the top of White Side, whose untidy cairn is reached next after a slight depression, is still grassy. It is the last for some time, as rock ridges, peaks and combes now fill the prospect. A short descent and longer climb up an exposed, stony ridge leads to Helvellyn Lower Man, joining a major path around the rim of Brown Cove on the left, which then slants across the last bit of the western slope of Helvellyn to the trig point and nearby four-sided windbreak. It is the seventh top, the highest, and usually the busiest, so the seats out of the wind in the shelter will surely all be occupied and you may as well continue around the rim of Nethermost Cove to a much quieter spot near the main cairn on Nethermost Pike before stopping for a snack. It is a good point from which to watch the almost endless ant-like procession along Striding Edge.

Spurn the broad track continuing south across the plateau unless visibility is poor, because it misses the marvellous views down the eastern combes seen from the path along the rim on your left. This has a little more rise and fall as it undulates over the buttress of High Crag and up to Dollywaggon Pike, but is infinitely preferable.

Ahead now is pain and apprehension, pain on the jolting descent down the steep slope to the south, rejoining the main track and heading for Grisedale Tarn, and apprehension at what you realise is ahead. For sticking strictly to AW's ridge-line involves not just climbing Fairfield but traversing Seat Sandal first as well. You could be forgiven for thinking of dabbling your feet in Grisedale Tarn then heading for the valley by way of Tongue Gill, but a short rest by the tarn and the consumption of another Mars Bar will generate enough energy to knock off Seat Sandal. To do so will mean contouring round the north side of the tarn and then picking a route beside the remnants of a collapsed wall leading up rough ground on the north side of the fell to its top. You don't *have* to take the direct line up the rough north slope unless you are a real purist; you could go right round Grisedale Tarn to Grisedale Hause and then just nip up to the cairn next to the collapsed wall on the top, then nip back down the same way – but of course I shouldn't suggest such a thought.

You will not nip up the next bit. This is the real toil after the pain, the climb up the west ridge of Fairfield. A slow but deliberate and continuous plod is the best way; just follow the cairns and the skittering paths up the scree and in due time you will reach embedded stones on a broad plateau, with its various shelters. The best spot for a peep down the splendid north face of Fairfield to the combes at the head of Deepdale is from the multi-chambered windbreak. Worth all the pain.

It's all downhill now; well, almost all. A line of cairns leads south from the summit and soon reaches grassier footing, leading along a fine ridge overlooking Rydale on the left and Tongue Gill on the right. A short rise, very short, leads to the big cairn on Great

Looking back to Nethermost Pike from Dollywaggon Pike over High Crag.

Rigg where you pause briefly at the cairn before swooping down easy rocks and then grass to where the ridge is almost level for quite a distance. The first distinctive little rocky point ahead is the un-named one above Erne Crag and the main path (as so often on this walk) by-passes it. The second little top, having a much smaller cairn on a quartzite outcrop, is Heron Pike. Now it really is downhill all the way home. You will probably not even be sure, or care, which cairn marks the top of Nab Scar as you pass by, but a steep descent now leads to tarmac and civilisation at Rydal Mount. Unless you arranged to be collected here, it will be best to turn left into the grounds of Rydal Hall and follow the signed path around the buildings and then through lovely parkland to join the A591 just outside Ambleside. I'm sorry the last bit is along the main road, but it is very short and all on the level. If you are lucky you will still find some of Ambleside's excellent tea shops open, and can enjoy a pot of tea and lots of sticky cakes. You've earned them.

Suitable escape points would be, first, from Helvellyn Lower Man going north-west down to the A591 beside Thirlmere via Helvellyn Gill; secondly, from Grisedale Tarn west to the A591 at Dunmail Raise.

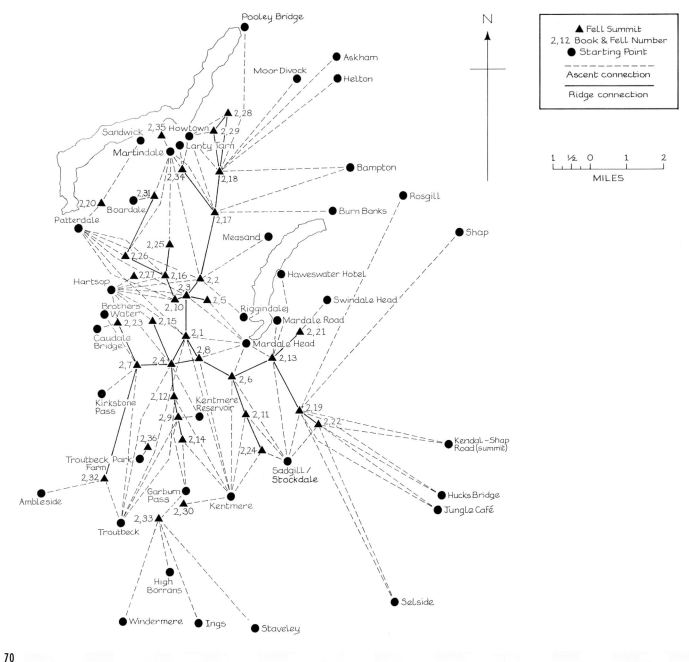

N

▲ Fell Summit
2,12 Book & Fell Number
● Starting Point
--- Ascent connection
—— Ridge connection

Pooley Bridge

Askham

Moor Divock

Helton

2,28

2,35 Howtown

Sandwick

2,29

Martindale

Lanty Tarn

Bampton

2,34

2,18

2,31

Boardale

2,20

Burn Banks

Patterdale

2,17

Rosgill

Shap

2,25

Measand

2,26

Haweswater Hotel

2,27

2,16

2,2

Hartsop

2,3

Swindale Head

Brothers
Water

2,10

2,5

Riggindale

2,23

2,15

Mardale Road

Caudale
Bridge

2,1

2,21

Mardale Head

2,8

2,7

2,4

2,13

Kirkstone
Pass

2,6

2,12

2,19

Kentmere
Reservoir

2,22

2,9

2,11

Kendal–Shap
Road (summit)

2,36

2,14

2,24

Troutbeck Park
Farm

Sadgill /
Stockdale

2,32

Hucks Bridge

Ambleside

Garburn
Pass

Jungle Café

2,33

2,30

Kentmere

High
Borrans

Selside

Windermere

Ings

Staveley

1 ½ 0   1   2
MILES

PART TWO

THE FAR EASTERN FELLS

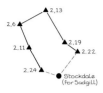

10 THE LONGSLEDDALE SKYLINE

BEST MAP: *OS 1:25 000 Outdoor Leisure 7, South Eastern area*
APPROXIMATE TIME: *6 hours*
TERRAIN: *Largely untracked on grass and peat in the early stages, joining good paths with boggy sections on the return.*

ITINERARY	Book & Fell No	Height of ascent	Distance	Cumulative distance	Height above sea level	
		feet	miles	miles	feet	mtrs
STOCKDALE					700	213
Grey Crag	2.22	1500	1.50	1.50	2093	638
Tarn Crag	2.19	250	0.75	2.25	2176	664
Branstree	2.13	700	1.75	4.00	2333	713
Harter Fell	2.06	700	2.00	6.00	2539	778
Kentmere Pike	2.11	150	1.25	7.25	2397	730
Shipman Knotts	2.24	80	1.25	8.50	1926	587
STOCKDALE				1.50	10.00	700	213
Totals of heights and distances		3380	10.00			

This circuit leads from what AW called the 'sombre attractiveness' of the eastern arm of Longsleddale to the 'exciting beauty that is typically Lakeland' as Mardale and Haweswater are reached. The first top on the round is Grey Crag, but AW's direct ascent from Sadgill Bridge via Great Howe is not very popular with the farmer at Sadgill and AW himself wrote: 'The first thousand feet is steep. In mist, the ascent has nothing to commend it! No path.' However Great Howe is a fine viewpoint and should be included in the route if possible. Fortunately the more direct Stockdale route, which AW found less attractive, can be combined with a visit to Great Howe, with better parking and an easier-angled ascent.

Reach Longsleddale by turning off the A6 Shap road about 4 miles north of Kendal then, near the head of the valley, turn right for the hamlet of Stockdale; here there is an outdoor pursuits centre and a café-cum-craft centre. Opposite the café there is a large parking space (grid ref 492054). A permissive way, to which I am advised there is no

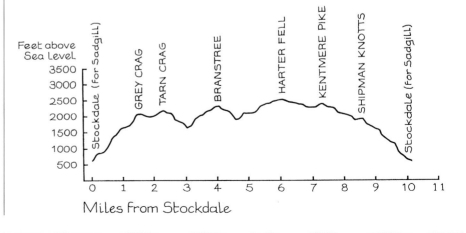

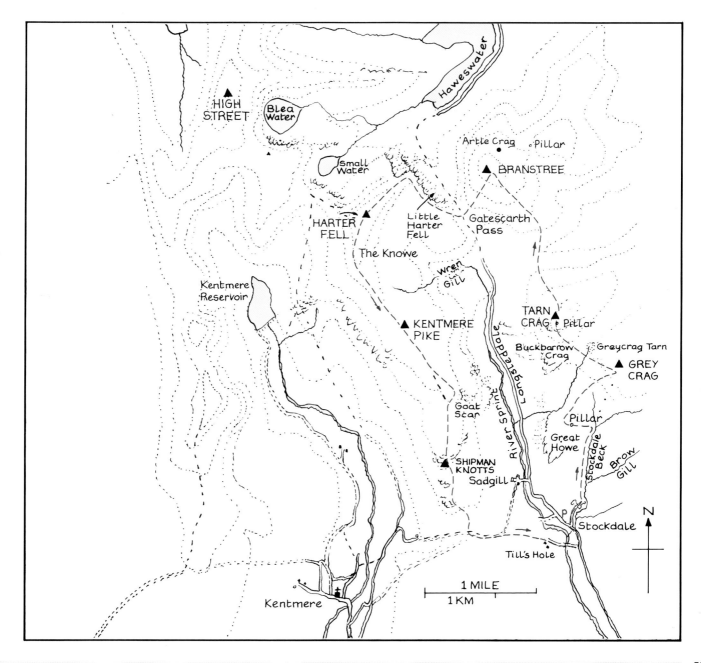

objection, leads up the lane past the buildings to the north-east, through a gate, then beside the beck to two gates reached just before the junction of Brow Gill (on the right) and Stockdale Beck. A turn through the left-hand gate and back sharp right beside Stockdale Beck (outside the fence on the right) leads to a gateway in the wall ahead, close to the stream (grid ref 492063). Now curve back left and uphill just a short way to the obvious wall-corner above and cross over here. There is no stile but *careful* use of large stones on the one side and a slope of earth and stones on the other, uphill, side make it a simple matter; then trend further left (west) to pass the first of a number of distinctive notched pillars, which were evidently constructed at the time the Haweswater Reservoir was being surveyed – the nick in the second one, higher up, aligns with the lower one and another will be seen later. Go a little further west and you find yourself on the grassy shoulder of Great Howe, with its splendid view up Longsleddale, dominated by the steep profile of Buckbarrow Crag; it is easy now to see why it was worth the diversion.

If you decide not to visit Great Howe, once you are through the gateway beside Stockdale Beck, the land continues rising in a sweep of grass slopes to Grey Crag, with only a wire fence or two to step over as the walls have been allowed to collapse. There is no path but the route is obvious.

Due north of Great Howe, on the skyline, is another survey pillar, on Tarn Crag, and that will shortly prove a most useful landmark. In the meantime, there is some almost flat moorland to trudge over, to the north-east, with just a wire fence to step over, followed by a gentle rise to the summit cairn on top of Grey Crag. It felt a very lonely and unvisited place on the last day I was there, that is until I spotted the lager cans stuffed into the cairn. Feeling irritated, I shoved them in my rucksack instead and then felt righteous, and much more able to enjoy the view. This is indeed remarkably extensive to the south and east, to the other Borrowdale, to the Howgills and to the Pennine country around Mallerstang. 'There is a vastness, a spaciousness, about it that is usually lacking in the views from Lakeland summits.'

The pillar on top of Tarn Crag to the north-west is the obvious next objective, and the ground ahead looks remarkably like Pennine moor, complete with groughs. Correct; apart from a few groughs you have to cross a broad and peaty depression holding the almost completely overgrown Greycrag Tarn, and then there is bog on the far side. The pillar is about 12ft high and, like the other two pillars on Great Howe, it has a slot on the top in line of sight of the higher of those. There are still a few spars scattered around, clearly the remains of the timber scaffolding which AW shows in his drawing made about forty years ago. The big cliffs of Buckbarrow Crag lower down are well hidden by the curve of fellside but to the north-west there is a glimpse of rugged country beyond the shoulder of Harter Fell; sadly the scar of the path worn up its flank is becoming intrusive.

Almost due north is the rounded grassy hump of Branstree, the next fell to be

Longsleddale seen from Great Howe.

visited, with the deep depression of the Gatescarth Pass between it and Harter Fell. Heading north now, a faint path is picked up beside the wire fence that descends the slope towards Branstree, over grass and peat-hags, to reach a minor hause between Longsleddale and Swindale. On the way down I met four walkers coming up: they were doing the Wainwright Tops and had thirteen left. I was impressed, they didn't look old enough. I've been walking the Lakeland fells for forty years and have only just completed the last few myself.

The fence continues uphill, but after the first steep rise it is reinforced by a substantial wall (where, in this wilderness of grass, did all the stone come from for such a solid construction?) as it traverses Selside Brow. This is a particularly dull ascent, enlivened a little by the glimpses of the abandoned Wrengill Quarry on the opposing slope. AW's comments about the abandoned cottages in Wrengill Quarry (with 'bedding, an extensive choice of domestic utensils, and firewood in plenty') suggest that he may well have spent a night or two there himself in his own youth, but he noted in 1957 that 'sheep have taken to dying in the living-rooms', making an open fellside bivouac more desirable.

The wall ends suddenly on the broad top of Branstree at a junction with a cross-fence and the actual summit is about 50 yards north of the wall, with a ground-level OS concrete circle and a few stones. About 300 yards to the north-east of the trig station and sitting in the surround of spiky rocks which AW identified from older maps as Artlecrag Pike but which the OS have since truncated to 'Artle Crag' is a fine, tall and unmistakable cairn which is worth inspection and from where there is a view of Haweswater, a view not seen from the main summit. East of this cairn is a little tarn in a depression and between it and the cairn, although hardly noticed and certainly not seen from the actual summit, is yet another of the survey pillars.

Shadowing the fence to the south-east from its junction with the wall on the top of Branstree, a path leads down to Gatescarth Pass, where an obvious track crosses the hause. In clear weather, the best view of the crags and gullies on the north-east face of Harter Fell is obtained from this descent, as well as a good view down the length of Longsleddale.

A well-worn path climbs from Gatescarth Pass up grass slopes, then levels and passes through a few rock outcrops on Little Harter Fell from where the first good views of Haweswater are obtained. It then runs alongside a substantial fence (obviously renewed since AW was here) which shortly takes a noticeable turn to the left, south-west. There is a boundary stone on this corner, with a chiselled letter 'H'; the nearby group of boulders is another good place from which to view both the full length of Haweswater and to get a tiny glint of light on Blea Water in its deep combe below the east-facing craggy slopes of High Street. Those views have not changed over the years, but on a Thursday, not a weekend, I could see from this same spot down to the car park at the head of Haweswater and it was full; that certainly is different.

Continuing south-west along the edge of the great drop, still rising gently and passing more cairns and another boundary stone, a single large cairn is reached on the top of Harter Fell. This, like the one passed earlier, is bristling with iron fence-posts. These, with what AW called their 'spectral weirdness', have been rusting away for as long as I can recall: a real mountain rubbish-tip.

Due west from the top of Harter Fell, a line of cairns leads off to the top of Nan Bield Pass, unseen from here, but the continuation of our ridge walk to Kentmere Pike is alongside the fence to the south, a simple promenade on a grassy path to The Knowe, easily passed without noticing although there is a slight change of direction here and an iron straining-post on the corner. Looking back, Nan Bield Pass is now visible. The continuation is gently downhill to a slight depression and then a rise up to Kentmere Pike where there is a scattering of embedded boulders. The trig point is over

Haweswater seen from Little Harter Fell.

the other side of the high wall and may be reached by a stile made of planks through it.

The path continuing downhill towards Shipman Knotts now initially follows the line of the fence heading just east of south but then leaves it to take a direct line and cut a corner. You should follow the fence, however, on a fainter path to reach a vantage point on Goat Scar, jutting out over Longsleddale. There is a cairn on the other side of a low wire fence, and a few rocks just beyond allow a grand view across the valley to Buckbarrow Crag, as well as giving glimpses of the steep eastern slopes of Kentmere Pike which would be otherwise unseen.

Returning to the main path, this continues beside the fence again to reach a ladder-stile over a wall traversing the fellside, then turns left alongside the wall to reach the noticeably rocky outcrops of Shipman Knotts. The path descends from here next to the wall and fairly sharply downhill, down a little defile formed by the wall on the left and outcrops on the right, but soon emerges onto easier grassy terrain although some boggy patches have to be negotiated. A last sharper descent down rocky steps reaches the bridleway between Kentmere and Sadgill. Turn left along this until the descent steepens, and a gate is reached beside some trees. Do not go through the gate, which will lead to Sadgill, but cross the ladder-stile just to its right. Descend the field beyond, with little trace of a path but beside the stream, to reach the farm at Till's Hole. An arrow-sign points the way through the farmyard; then cross the River Sprint by the farm track which leads to the main valley road again. Turn right here for 200 yards or so and then a left turn leads directly back to Stockdale.

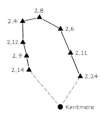

11 THE KENTMERE ROUND

BEST MAP: *OS 1:25 000 Outdoor Leisure 7, South Eastern area*
APPROXIMATE TIME: *6–7 hours*
TERRAIN: *Easy underfoot but sometimes boggy, with occasional rocky ground and a pathless descent on grass.*

ITINERARY	Book & Fell No	Height of ascent	Distance	Cumulative distance	Height above sea level	
		feet	miles	miles	feet	mtrs
KENTMERE					525	160
Shipman Knotts	2.24	1400	2.25	2.25	1926	587
Kentmere Pike	2.11	525	1.25	3.50	2397	730
Harter Fell	2.06	275	1.25	4.75	2539	778
Mardale Ill Bell	2.08	450	1.00	5.75	2496	761
Thornthwaite Crag	2.04	250	1.33	7.08	2569	784
Froswick	2.12	300	1.00	8.08	2359	720
Ill Bell	2.09	400	0.67	8.75	2476	757
Yoke	2.14	130	0.67	9.42	2309	706
KENTMERE			2.50	11.92	525	160
Totals of heights and distances		3730	11.92			

This is a classic Lake District horseshoe, although a reversal of one of AW's ascents to Yoke can give a more interesting and less obvious return to the valley than is usually taken. I propose an anti-clockwise direction for the walk as the peaks forming the dramatic east wall of Kentmere will be best seen in the morning from the ridge to Kentmere Pike. The first top is Shipman Knotts, which I mention because many walkers seem to think they've done this round when they have started with Kentmere Pike.

There are very few parking places in Kentmere except opposite St Cuthbert's Church in Kentmere (grid ref 456041), about four miles north of Staveley, so it will pay to arrive early. You could then just blast off and walk up the mile of road from Kentmere via Green Quarter to the start of the old bridleway between Kentmere and Longsleddale, but the following route is pleasanter.

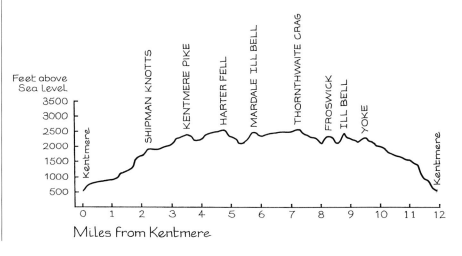

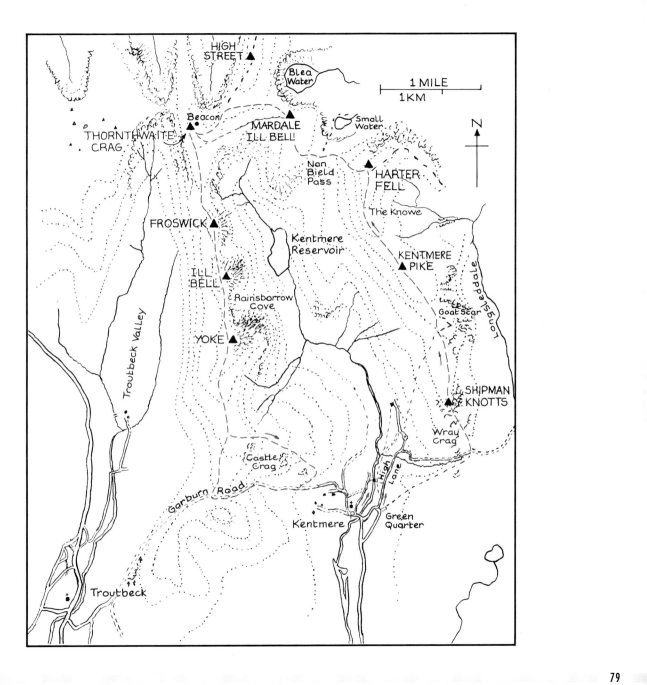

Go round the church to its right side, as you face it, and follow a good track (footpath signs and yellow arrows) heading north-east, keeping right at the fork and following a walled lane through several gateways. Watch carefully for a stone slit-stile on the right, just before a gate ahead, and turn through this and down to a footbridge over the River Kent. The path beyond winds round a hillock and up to another stile on the edge of a walled lane. Cross the lane to another stile and continue up the field beyond to reach High Lane. Go left along this, through a gate, then turn uphill to the right at a sign 'Public Byway Sadgill and Longsleddale'.

This is a good track rising up a walled lane until the walls diverge at a gate, then shortly passing beneath some rock knuckles seen up on the fellside to the left (Wray Crag) to reach a gate at a wall corner. Here leave the track and turn up the slope on the left, on a path rising over boggy ground and with a wall on the right. This path soon picks a way more steeply up rock steps at the right-hand end of Wray Crag. More level ground follows, the path still shadowing the wall except where it drifts away in attempts to choose firmer ground, but it then hugs the wall closely as it skirts just to the right of an outcrop and climbs to a cairn on Shipman Knotts immediately above it. More level ground follows, to a ladder-stile over the main intake wall. The path continues on the other side, slanting away rightwards from the wall, but a wire fence also leads uphill from this point to reach Goat Scar. A step over the fence where it turns a corner leads to a cairn on the rock outcrops of Goat Scar; this is a good viewpoint to Branstree at the head of Longsleddale and to Buckbarrow's crags across its depths.

Returning to the fence and following it north-westwards, the main path is soon rejoined, gingerly negotiating some boggy ground and then rising up a long and peaty slope, the fence giving way to a wall just before the top of the slope, which continues up the remainder of the rise to reach Kentmere Pike. There is no great feeling of being on a peak here, just a scattering of embedded rocks, with the trig point hiding over the wall on the right. Yoke, Ill Bell and Froswick are now more clearly in sight across upper Kentmere on the left but a slight descent is needed to bring Kentmere Reservoir into the picture.

A gradual descent from the Pike follows, across some evil peat groughs in the depression beside the wall, then a fence again takes over on the steady plod up to The Knowe, where there is an old iron straining-post on the elbow bend. At last, the peaty going is left behind. Ahead is a large cairn, bristling with old iron fence-posts, marking the highest point on the almost flat-topped Harter Fell.

From here, anticipation quickens into excitement as you turn to the north-west across a bare slope marked by cairns to the top of the ridge leading to Nan Bield Pass. Rocks, after all that peat, lead sharply down and onto a level top from where high crags drop away on the north side. Then stony slopes wind down in a series of steps to reach the dramatic notch of the pass. From here there is a splendid view down to Kentmere

Looking back to Harter Fell and Nan Bield Pass from Mardale Ill Bell.

Reservoir and the soaring ridge high above it along which this walk will continue. The winds can blast exuberantly through here and the stone shelter built in the gap, a short length of wall with two collapsing arms extended towards Haweswater, may be appreciated for a short stop. Continue on the path which goes to the left of a small out-crop before tackling a stony slope beyond and which slants right towards Mardale Ill Bell. On this climb there are equally fine views to the north, with one memorable one in particular when Small Water and the head of Haweswater come into view one above the other. Then more stony ground, passing some small outcrops of flat-topped square rocks, leads to the summit cairn.

From Mardale Ill Bell the broad dome of High Street dominates the view ahead, but our path is west to Thornthwaite Crag and its beacon. The main path leaving Mardale Ill Bell is well-grooved in the peat and contours across the broad southern slopes of High Street, reaching the wall along its spine. A turn left here beside the wall soon leads to the line of the old Roman road and this then curves right and slightly upwards to the tall beacon on Thornthwaite Crag. An alternative path may be noticed closely following the rim round the head of Hall Cove above Kentmere, and in clear weather this is a more interesting route. But it is uncairned, passes through some very boggy patches and changes direction several times, which can cause confusion in mist or snow. As walkers have found to their cost in the past, it is easy to get lost up here in such conditions.

I walked this round one March day, and from the valley could only see cloud on the tops. Once I was in it, it became a mixture of howling wind and sleet and on High Street there was saturated slush above ankle height so my boots were soon soaked. Visibility was about 20 yards and the paths were non-existent. The wind-chill factor was obviously very high and I had forgotten the little windproof coats that I have made for my dogs so I cut holes in a couple of plastic bags and popped these on them instead. Ten minutes later I suddenly realised I was missing one of them and so reversed my footsteps. I found Freddie standing forlornly, his plastic bag blown to tatters, and shivering violently so it was into the rucksack with him immediately. I retreated to Nan Bield Pass and went down the valley route to Kentmere and the little dog just snuggled down until we were back at the car.

Leaving Thornthwaite Beacon, the return half of the walk is over the pointed tops of Froswick and Ill Bell seen so well from the other side of the Kentmere valley. The way is initially to the SSE beside a collapsed wall for a short way, but when it turns left (and shortly ends) the path continues along the line of an old fence gradually descending towards the narrowing grassy ridge which quickly rises to the top of Froswick. Ahead now is the fine cone of Ill Bell, its steep rocky eastern slope falling sheer to Kentmere Reservoir, rising beyond another hause which is also soon reached. But then a longer and much stonier rise, during which the effects of the day's exertions will surely be felt, curves with a right hook up to the main cairn amidst the rocks on the top of Ill Bell. Although exposed, this is a fine perch for views back along this grand ridge to the beacon, to Nan Bield Pass and to Harter Fell. Looking south, the glint of light will be seen on Windermere beyond the Troutbeck valley. The main cairn is not alone, however: a second large one is nearby, with a circular windbreak at its base, while a third is just a few paces south. These three can be seen from many surrounding fells and are often used to confirm its identity, but I can foresee some confusion in the future if any of the mini-cairns which are also sprouting here grow to maturity.

From the last main cairn the path continues fairly steeply downhill on the rim of Rainsborrow Cove, whose fierce inclines fall to the Kentmere valley floor far below, then curves up gradually past various iron straining-posts to reach a cairn on a stony outcrop marking the top of Yoke. This doesn't look like a very exciting summit, but the east face of Yoke is made up largely of the enormous broken rock buttresses of Rainsborrow Crag. Nothing will be sensed of these unless a short walk is taken from the summit to the east, when a little tarn will be found at the top of a long broken ridge separating Rainsborrow Cove from Rainsborrow Crag and better views will be gained from here. This ridge incidentally gives a good scrambling ascent from the Kentmere valley to be remembered for another day.

The descent path from Yoke passes another large cairn from where there is another long-range view to Windermere, then trends downhill to the level where a fainter path, a direct route from Ill Bell, comes in from the right. Continuing on the level for a short distance, the now shaly path swings left and descends quite sharply across fellside to reach a main intake wall at a ladder-stile (grid ref 436060).

Froswick and Ill Bell seen from the rim path near Gavel Crag.

This is a moment of decision: cross for the tourist route, don't cross for AW's route back to Kentmere. If you cross, this intake wall continues along the broad and peaty crest of the ridge. The path starts by shadowing the wall but then trends away to the right over very peaty ground, and also away from Kentmere. If taken, it does become clearer along a grassy track followed by cairns across another peaty stretch, leading finally to the Garburn Road which links Kentmere with Troutbeck. A left turn here will lead with certainty to Kentmere.

A more attractive, although obviously very little-used alternative, a reverse of AW's ascent route to Yoke, is not to cross the intake wall but to keep on its left side, passing a wire-and-posts sheep-pen beside it. Step over this and then head east, over undulating ground with numerous small outcrops until you cross a collapsed wall. Turn downhill now, south-east, with some attractive views back up Kentmere, into the funnel formed by two walls. Passing just north of Castle Crag and Piked Howes and beside a little stream, this route descends to where a right turn leads through a gateway and along a grassy track to the south-west below Ewe Crags to the Garburn Road. A left turn here leads through the gate into a walled lane. This passes the Badger Rock on the right, then one more gate leads to the tarmac track back to Kentmere Church.

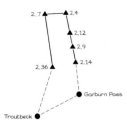

12 THE TROUTBECK CIRCUIT

BEST MAP: *OS 1:25 000 Outdoor Leisure 7, South Eastern area*
APPROXIMATE TIME: *6–7 hours*
TERRAIN: *Stony then boggy paths lead to the high ground, then mixed ground including steep shale leads to a rougher but essentially grassy descent.*

ITINERARY	Book & Fell No	Height of ascent	Distance	Cumulative distance	Height above sea level	
		feet	miles	miles	feet	mtrs
TROUTBECK					850	259
Garburn Pass		900	2.25	2.25	1475	450
Yoke	2.14	850	1.75	4.00	2309	706
Ill Bell	2.09	300	0.67	4.67	2476	757
Froswick	2.12	285	0.67	5.34	2359	720
Thornthwaite Crag	2.04	480	1.00	6.34	2569	784
Caudale Moor	2.07	560	1.00	7.34	2502	763
Troutbeck Tongue	2.36	215	2.50	9.84	1191	364
TROUTBECK			3.00	12.84	850	259
Totals of heights and distances		3590	12.84			

To stick strictly to AW's ridge-line network on this round will quite definitely take you onto private land on the approach to Wansfell where the 'Keep Out' and 'Private' signs do not allow much compromise, so I have devised an alternative finish which I consider is better anyway.

The start is at Troutbeck and, apart from a few individual places, there is parking space for about six cars on the side road beside the Trout Beck just off the A592 (Kirkstone Pass road) where it crosses Church Bridge (grid ref 413027). Back at the main road, turn right (south) over Church Bridge, then up the first track on the left, a stony way beneath trees. This is the Garburn Road, the old bridleway to Kentmere. It winds up between stone walls which restrict any views for a while, but the wall on the left soon gives way to a wire fence and then there's a grand view up the Troutbeck valley with most of the round now visible. This pleasant 'road' slants across fellside, crossing two transverse tracks, above the cabins and caravans on the immaculate Limefitt Park site, to a gate with a plantation just beyond on the right. The trees partly hide some huge spoil

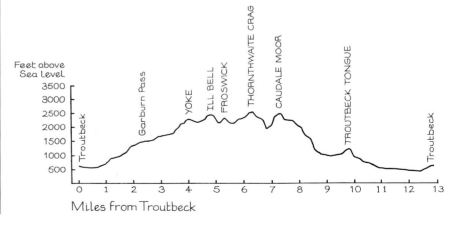

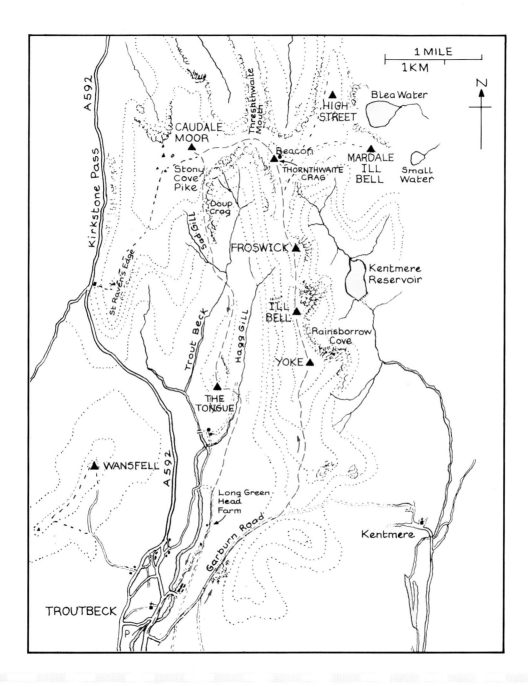

tips from former quarrying operations. A little further up, the wire fence reverts to a wall but it is low enough to see over easily and for sheep to skip over it with impunity; it doesn't seem to have much point. At about 1000ft above the valley there is another gate; shortly beyond that the wall on the left comes to an end and the track descends slightly to an elbow bend. Here, just before the top of the Garburn Pass and where you can just walk off the track onto open fell, our path heads off left (north), cairned with distinctive white stones. These lead across some boggy ground but then the path is along a pleasant grassy and almost level promenade for a quarter-mile before it rises noticeably and then slants across more peaty and boggy ground to reach the main wall running along the spine of the ridge.

The path now rises on the left-hand side of the wall to cross it at a ladder-stile at the point where the wall curves away to the left around the flank of Yoke. Beyond the stile, the shaly path curves to the right a little and then upwards before the ground levels off briefly. Here a slighter path leads to the left, making directly for Ill Bell and avoiding Yoke entirely. Surely it could only possibly be used by exhausted walkers returning, not advancing, in bad weather? (I am always charitable in such matters.) The main path climbs a little higher to reach a large cairn (a better viewpoint than the summit), then the ground rises very gradually for a further 150 yards to reach another cairn, this time on a stony outcrop. This is the summit of Yoke. A few rusty iron fence-posts lying on the ground are all that remains of AW's 'wire fence forming a right-angle nearby'.

Continuing north from Yoke, a slight descent leads past three iron straining-posts, remains of a fence that once ran along the ridge, and the path confidently skirts the edge of Star Crag's very steep ground on the right, from where there is a dramatic view down to Kentmere Reservoir. Continuing around the rim of the equally fierce slopes of Rainsborrow Cove, a fairly sharp rise then follows up a stony path to reach Ill Bell, recognisable even from considerable distances for its distinctive bell-like shape and for its three large cairns. One of these is perched on a rocky base with a stone windbreak at its foot and you may struggle to fold your map while you knock over your thermos flask here as well as anywhere else. The main cairn is also on rocks, surveying a fine view along the continuing ridge ahead.

A stony descent, passing the summit rocks of Ill Bell on their left, leads to a col and then up to the smaller but still shapely cone of Froswick. A descent then a rise to a new level, then a further rise reaches a parting of ways. Occasional fence-posts have marked the route along the ridge so far, but at this point there is a straining-post with two more posts very close to it (an old gateway). Immediately beyond this gateway (which is a very useful landmark in bad conditions) and while still rising, the path forks, the right branch curving round a steep and shaly gully to the side of the broken rocks of Gavel Crag. The left branch, the one needed, heads for the tall stone pillar of Thornthwaite Beacon, seen ahead above the stony slopes of Thornthwaite Crag.

Looking back along the ridge to Froswick and Ill Bell from Thornthwaite Beacon.

As I was approaching the beacon four or five huge fellhounds came streaking out of nowhere and disappeared as quickly, baying as they went. The sound then died away for a few minutes, but as I left the beacon I heard it again, rising in intensity and coming from the direction of Stony Cove half a mile away. When it suddenly stopped completely I assumed that a fox had met its end. Better than dying a slow death from poison or a gunshot wound.

Following the wall off to the north-west from the beacon, the main path soon begins the loose, shaly descent to the col of Threshthwaite Mouth, shadowing the now-

Looking back to Froswick, Ill Bell and Yoke from Stony Cove Pike.

collapsed wall. In places, the descent is in zigzags, easing what can be an awkward passage in winter conditions. From the hause, there are long-ranging views to the north down Pasture Beck, the lowest fellsides dappled with drumlins and the farthest slopes stretching to Ullswater. To the south, grassier inclines on the Hagg Gill flanks of Froswick, Ill Bell and Yoke give little hint of their fierce eastern combes, whose crests were traversed such a short time ago. The climb from Threshthwaite Mouth is a stiff pull up a rocky slope with two little steps of easy scrambling. The path stays close to the disintegrating wall on the right until, as the angle eases, the wall runs into a corner ahead.

The older OS maps name Stony Cove, although the newer ones do not, and the path slants south-west to a large cairn marking the top of Stony Cove Pike directly above the cove itself. There are good views from here to Kidsty Pike and High Street in the north-east. To the south-west, passing a smaller cairn, is a wall-corner, from where one wall (collapsed) runs due south and another runs west. The main path goes through a gap in the corner and, via St Raven's Edge, towards Kirkstone Pass. AW's ridge-line continues to Wansfell but to go that way involves climbing two walls, crossing two more, almost certainly getting your feet wet and ignoring obvious 'Keep Out' and 'Private' signs. It is also, as AW wrote and I can confirm, 'a long, uninteresting trudge'. Much better to forget it.

The alternative return that I suggest begins from the wall-corner close to the cairn on Stony Cove Pike, mentioned above, and is, in all essentials, the reverse of one of AW's ascent routes to Caudale Moor. The collapsed wall to the south runs above a line of crags (one of which is Doup Crag) which overlook the valley of the Trout Beck and form a clearly defined ridge, and this is used for the descent. There is a faint path on the east side of this wall (left, looking down). Lower down, the wall is in excellent condition and it forms a junction with another which is in equally good condition. AW seems to have climbed this wall, but there is no need: simply turn left down beside the transverse wall towards Trout Beck and cross it by using one of the numerous gaps found in it as soon as the slope steepens. Now continue south to reach the several streams flowing down Sad Gill (not named on the later OS maps). Cross these above the cascades and continue down brackeny fellside to reach the indistinct valley path between Threshthwaite Mouth and Ing Bridge (Troutbeck). This path could be followed south, of course, and if the water is too high to ford the Trout Beck, there will be no alternative but to use it, staying on the west bank and crossing by the little packhorse bridge further down the valley. But if the Trout Beck is fordable, an opportunity is presented to return along the ridge of The Tongue, thus also bagging another 'Wainwright Top', but in any event enjoying more pleasing views and an interesting descent.

Having crossed Trout Beck, which is usually easy, cross to where a gate in the intake wall around the head of the valley gives access to a sheepfold and thus also to the northern roots of The Tongue. These are fairly smothered in rushes and the first of two

Looking back up Hagg Gill from the foot of The Tongue.

ancient cairns is simply a heap of stones almost buried in them, but the second is more obvious on a little rise and the double chamber that AW illustrated is still the same although the nearby tree has given up the ghost. The broad ridge leads, with some effort over the rough ground, to easier grassier terrain, stepping over a low wire fence and continuing gradually uphill to the small cairn on the highest point.

This is a splendid viewpoint down the Troutbeck valley to Windermere and worth enjoying before locating the curving spine of an easy rock ridge leading south downhill. Another low wire fence is crossed easily low down the ridge and when the intake wall is met a turn to the left alongside it quickly leads to the main path (heading up Hagg Gill) at a gate. Go through this but then turn down the slope to the beck on the left, crossing it by a footbridge. A stile and gate then enable the old bridleway down the east side of Hagg Gill to be used down the valley. This leads easily and very gradually downhill through sheep and cow pastures, with a firmer section underfoot near Long Green Head Farm, and a last very pleasant stretch before turning right just past a gate and down the slope into the Limefitt Park site. The path is signed across this, reaching the main road again just north of Church Bridge and only minutes away from the car.

Hartsop

2,23   2,15

2,7   2,4

13 THE PASTURE BECK RIM

BEST MAP: *OS 1:25 000 Outdoor Leisure 5, North Eastern area*
APPROXIMATE TIME: *4½ hours*
TERRAIN: *Mostly on good firm paths with some steep scree mid-walk and a very steep descent on grass at the finish.*

ITINERARY	Book & Fell No	Height of ascent	Distance	Cumulative distance	Height above sea level	
		feet	miles	miles	feet	mtrs
HARTSOP					700	213
Hartsop Dodd	2.23	1450	1.25	1.25	2018	618
Caudale Moor	2.07	620	1.33	2.58	2502	763
Thornthwaite Crag	2.04	620	1.00	3.58	2569	784
Gray Crag	2.15	150	1.25	4.83	2286	699
HARTSOP			2.00	6.83	700	213
Totals of heights and distances		2840	6.83			

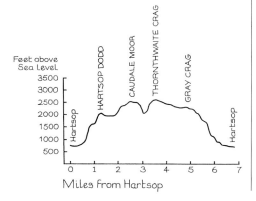

Feet above Sea Level

Miles from Hartsop

The imposing front of Hartsop Dodd as seen from Hartsop village, looking like a 'steep-sided conical hill' is, as AW points out, a sham since it is 'no more than the knuckled fist at the end of one of the several arms of Caudale Moor'. The ascent of the fell by its north ridge which faces Hartsop is, however, the start of a short round of considerable interest, a high-level tour of the skyline of Pasture Beck. If misty conditions develop on the top of Caudale Moor, it will be well to avoid any of the deviations I have suggested in the text.

The best parking is at the far end of the attractive village of Hartsop, reached by turning off the A592 about 5 miles north of Troutbeck or 2 miles south of Patterdale (grid ref 410131). Alternative parking may be found at Cow Bridge, where the A592 crosses the Goldrill Beck just north of Brothers Water (grid ref 403134).

From the car park in the village, go through the gate enclosing it and turn right (public footpath sign for Pasture Beck), crossing the bridge over the beck and making directly towards the base of the north ridge of Hartsop Dodd, which challenges you directly ahead. At a gate and stile, the path up Pasture Beck turns left (south-east) but instead continue directly ahead up the wallside to a stile in the wall corner, then very steeply in the same direction to a shoulder on the north ridge; here you can catch your breath and tuck your shirt back in. If you need any more excuses for a halt, there is also a good view down Patterdale.

A steep but really delightful path now leads up the north ridge, not so much zigzagging as insinuating its way, like the wriggles of a snake, up a series of grassy and occasionally stony grooves which end just before reaching a single three-legged iron fence-post just beyond a shoulder. The angle eases, you pass a second post and reach a last sharp pull uphill towards the summit cairn. When you arrive, it proves to be just the end of a stone wall and the real cairn of collapsed stones is just a little further, beside the wall.

There's a good view over Dovedale to Dove Crag, Hart Crag and Fairfield in morning light, when Gray Crag to the east is usually little more than an outline, but the

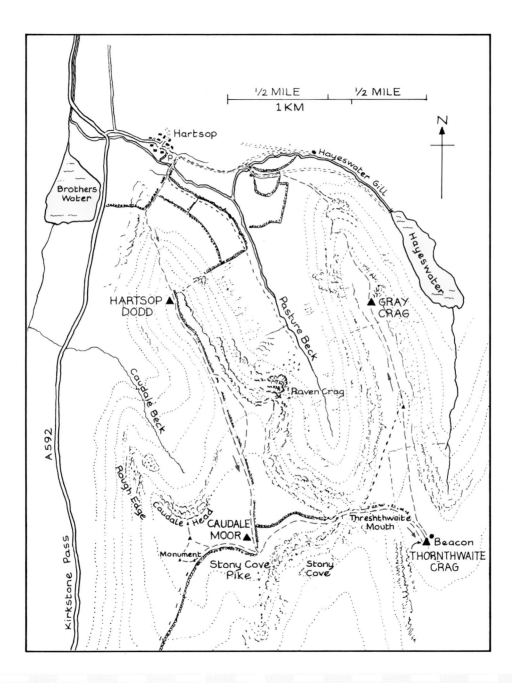

Hartsop and Patterdale from the north ridge of Hartsop Dodd.

view ahead (south) is dominated by Red Screes and Rough Edge rising to Caudale Moor. There is no possibility of losing the way for the path shadows the wall linking Hartsop Dodd with Caudale Moor, but the wall now has many breaches in it and, as AW suggests – although it appears few follow his suggestion – much better views are gained by deviating from it and walking instead along the edge of the escarpment overlooking Raven Crag and Pasture Beck. The footpath sticks closely to the wall until it rises onto a broad, flat top and a large cairn is reached, the first of a number.

You might not bother much about cairns: the big ones mark the top, don't they?

And I didn't either until I started to realise that *some people* take them very seriously indeed. Well, I've now realised that there is a bit of a puzzle about the cairns on the broad expanse of Caudale Moor and they have been multiplying since AW drew his map; furthermore, the OS maps at 1:25 000 and 1:50 000 show Caudale Moor in different places. However, this first cairn is undoubtedly on the highest land, inside the 760m contour and as the highest spot height in the area is given as 763m/2503ft, this has to be the highest point of Caudale Moor. Now I am aware that I may have AW's ethereal presence coming to haunt me for saying so but I don't think the highest point of the Moor is the same thing as Stony Cove Pike, as he suggests. Only about 100 yards away to the south-east and just beside the well-marked path rising from the hause of Threshthwaite Mouth to the east, is another large cairn, on slightly *lower* ground. This is at the end of a long ridge running south above Doup Crag and down towards Troutbeck and it also overlooks the rocky cirque of Stony Cove (named on the older 1:25 000 maps). Clearly this identifies Stony Cove Pike and is a good viewpoint to the Froswick–Ill Bell ridge across Trout Beck; the higher cairn surely marks the top of Caudale Moor.

These perhaps academic considerations apart, whilst up here and before descending to Threshthwaite Mouth, and if time and weather permit, it is well worth making a small diversion, but this time for the view. Take the path heading west instead of east; you pass another smaller cairn first and then go through a gap in the collapsed wall corner only fifty paces from it. Now walk alongside the remains of the wall also heading west. Over a slight rise, a tarn (in fact, two tarns, although only one is immediately visible) comes into view in a depression ahead and beyond that is another large cairn on a rounded sky-line. You will need to turn off the main path, which stays alongside the collapsed wall, to reach it, but I do urge you to do so to enjoy the grand view that will shortly follow. This cairn is smack in the middle of the area marked on the OS 1:25 000 map as 'Caudale Moor', thus adding to this man-made confusion, but only about 100 yards away to the north-west and slightly lower is yet another well-built cairn. This one is un-mistakably at the head of a geographical feature that everybody recognises: the fine cirque of rocks and scree called Caudale Head, at the head of Caudale Beck. There is a splendid view from here down to Brothers Water, with Rough Edge bounding the left of the cirque and the right arm stretching back to Hartsop Dodd.

Return to the main path (south-east from Caudale Head) beside the collapsed wall until it reaches a corner where it turns SSW for the Kirkstone Pass. About 200 yards south-west from here (and a little footpath leads to it) is yet one more mound of stones crowned by a simple wooden cross: this is different, it is Mark Atkinson's monument. A simple stone plaque is set into the mound and carved with the words: 'Hic jacet Mark Atkinson of Kirkstone Pass Inn, died 14 June 1930 aged 69 years'. Next to it is another plaque: 'Also his son William Ion Atkinson, died 2nd April 1987 aged 83 years'. The

Hartsop Dodd seen from Caudale Head.

spot was obviously chosen so that the Atkinsons could keep an eye on the pub and see that nobody nips off without paying, for it is well in sight from here.

All wanderings on Caudale Moor now completed, take the path returning past the tarns, past the cairn on Stony Cove Pike and descend eastwards to the hause of Threshthwaite Mouth which forms the pass between the valleys of Troutbeck on the south and Pasture Beck on the north. The path follows the line taken by a collapsed wall into the gap and the tall rock pillar of Thornthwaite Beacon will normally be clearly visible on the edge of the scarp of Thornthwaite Crag on the far side. Slabs of knobbly rock and a couple of very short rock walls may require a touch of hands for balance on the descent, but the further you descend the less enticing does the obvious re-ascent look, especially as it is clearly on loose scree in the upper half. However, unless it is either very wet or iced, when its ascent may need great care, the climb will be simple enough if tiring and a well-used path, shadowing a largely collapsed wall, leads to the great

Thornthwaite Beacon. This is a well-built rock pillar that has acted as yet another irresistible place for countless lunches.

Heading north now, a faint trod soon develops along the mostly grassy spine leading out towards Gray Crag, crossing the remains of a wall, with good views down to Hayeswater. A slight rise leads to a first cairn and then a gentle descent and re-ascent follows, now with good views down Pasture Beck on the left side and with the striking buttresses of Raven Crag, only partly seen from the Hartsop Dodd ridge, now seen in more detail. It is not surprising that the rock-climbing routes on that crag are of a high order of difficulty. Just beyond a second collapsed wall is the second cairn, on Gray Crag's summit, the last high point of the round.

A delightful descent now follows, with splendid views across Hayeswater Gill to the fells around Angle Tarn. I was lucky enough to catch low-angle declining sun setting them aflame; and although I caught a couple of shots, the light had gone before I had time to change the film.

An obvious path on grass leads down the spine of the north ridge as far as a shoulder. From here the way becomes steeper but still obvious, crosses first one little transverse path created by sheep (it runs out into grass at each end) and then reaches a second transverse path, where it stops dead on the edge of even steeper ground, so it is just as well. Promenade to the left along this second path, like the sheep, but only for a dozen paces and then make for a line of pocket-holds descending in a slanting line to the right. These lead down more steep grassy ground to a point just below a little crag, after which decreasingly steep slopes lead to a junction with the main path from Hayeswater. A left turn here down the stony path soon leads to the footbridge over Hayeswater Gill and the Hartsop car park again.

Mark Atkinson's Monument on Caudale Moor.

14 THE HAYESWATER HORIZON

BEST MAP: *OS 1:25 000 Outdoor Leisure 5, North Eastern area*
APPROXIMATE TIME: *6¼ hours*
TERRAIN: *A trackless ascent on grass, then good paths on firm ground for almost all the rest of the round.*

ITINERARY	Book & Fell No	Height of ascent	Distance	Cumulative distance	Height above sea level	
		feet	miles	miles	feet	mtrs
HARTSOP					700	213
Gray Crag	2.15	1800	2.00	2.00	2286	699
Thornthwaite Crag	2.04	350	1.25	3.25	2569	784
High Street	2.01	250	1.25	4.50	2718	828
Rampsgill Head	2.03	250	1.25	5.75	2581	792
The Knott	2.10	65	0.33	6.08	2423	739
Rest Dodd	2.16	360	0.75	6.83	2278	696
Angletarn Pikes	2.26	300	1.75	8.58	1857	565
HARTSOP			2.75	11.33	700	213
Totals of heights and distances		3375	11.33			

The 'lofty ridge, bounded by exceedingly steep flanks' of Gray Crag is the start of this circuit of the high land above Hayeswater Reservoir, but the ridges lead on to give views also of Blea Water, Haweswater and Angle Tarn. The first ascent is the hardest; the return is delightful.

The best parking is as for Walk 13, either at the far end of Hartsop village (grid ref 410131) reached by turning off the A592 about 5 miles north of Troutbeck or 2 miles south of Patterdale. Alternative parking may be found at Cow Bridge, where the A592 crosses the Goldrill Beck just north of Brothers Water (grid ref 403134).

From the Hartsop car park, go through the gate and take the obvious track ahead to the east, signed 'Bridleway Hayeswater', passing sheep-pens on the right and with the steep west flank and nose of Gray Crag seen directly ahead, separating Hayeswater Gill from Pasture Beck. The tarmac strip continues beyond a gate/cattle-grid to the filter house for the reservoir, but turn off to the right on a lower, rougher track and cross

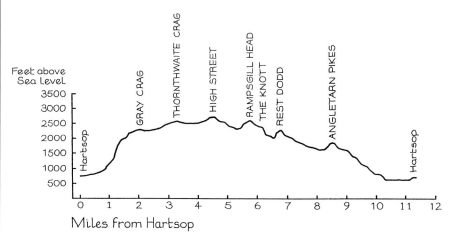

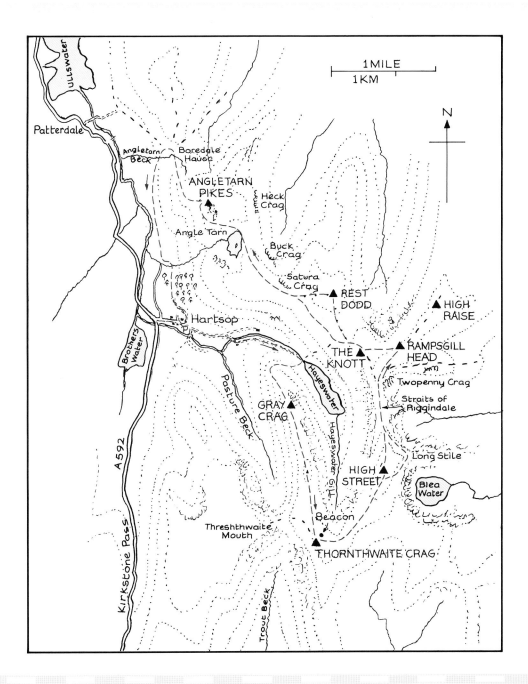

Looking along the Gray Crag ridge from near Thornthwaite Crag.

Hayeswater Gill by a farm bridge (no longer the simple stone slab that AW illustrated). This track rises uphill past a barn, up a wide walled lane to a gate and then up the right bank of the gill. Grass slopes, rearing more steeply upwards as they rise, stretch towards Gray Crag on the right of the path. You might just be tempted to go that way for there is a sketchy path but it is extremely steep and normally used only as a descent. The easier way in ascent, as AW points out, is to continue to the dam at Hayeswater and then gain the ridge from there by a slanting line out to the right.

Few walkers seem to have taken this good advice as there is no sign of foot-traffic up the grass slopes from the dam to the shoulder on the north ridge and it is probably the absence of walkers on Gray Crag generally which encourages a few deer to frequent the Pasture Beck slopes of the fell; a quiet approach will often disclose them grazing quietly and I have seen what I guess to be the same small herd now for a number of years.

A path leads up the grassy but fairly sharp ridge now rising ahead over a couple of small humps to a high point on top of a small crag overlooking Hayeswater; this is a better spot than the top since the cairn on Gray Crag summit, a hundred paces further on, has no view of the reservoir at all. Continuing along the spine of the ridge and shortly crossing a collapsed wall, the faint path leads to a slight depression and rise beyond to a second cairn, then crosses a second collapsed wall, after which it continues close to the edge of scree tongues leading down towards Hayeswater on the left side of the ridge. It fades on the rising stonier ground towards Thornthwaite Crag ahead, but the wall rising from Threshthwaite Mouth appears on the right hand and leads quickly to Thornthwaite Beacon, standing like a tower on the ramparts of a castle.

From here an obvious scarred path swings away to the north-east, round the head of Hayeswater Gill, towards the broad slopes of High Street; the line of the old fence mentioned by AW is hardly detectable any more and is no longer necessary. This newer path soon cuts through a collapsed transverse wall just fifty paces left of a wall corner. From this corner, a wall in much better repair traverses the length of High Street but the main path follows a much older course – that of the old Roman road. The marching legions were obviously too busy keeping in step and avoiding extra fatigues like cleaning out the latrines to be concerned about the beauty of the landscape, simply choosing the shortest route. Initially this allows only longer-range views to the north and west but as it rises it skirts closer to the edge on the left, allowing peeps across to Gray Crag and down the grey scree slopes to Hayeswater, a long way below. Shortly it begins a long but gentle decline, completely by-passing the actual summit, and after traversing entirely across the flank of High Street, only rejoins the main line of the ridge at the narrow hause of the Straits of Riggindale. It is a fast crossing, but avoids all the best of High Street.

I suggest, therefore, that instead of tramping along the course of the Roman road, stay close to the wall and shadow it over the top of the fell. This may well be 'barren of scenic interest" but it is where horse races and other junketings were regularly held not so long ago. Go past the trig point beside the wall and continue down the northern slope. Then at last the tremendous prospect down the east face of High Street is revealed on the right, with its two deep combes. The right-hand one contains Blea Water, separated by the straight rock ridge of Long Stile which is, in my opinion, the finest possible way up to High Street. Ahead, the collapsed wall snakes down the ridge to the Straits of Riggindale, overlooked by the grey rocks of Twopenny Crag, where it is joined by the Roman road.

After leaving the Straits, with its view down to the right to Haweswater, the main

High Street seen from Thornthwaite Beacon.

path leads directly ahead towards The Knott, but Wainwright's ridge-line (as described in the Pictorial Guide) leads first, a little surprisingly, to Rampsgill Head. Surprisingly, because it appears such an indefinite place, but correctly because, as he points out, it is 'geographically a "key" point in the High Street range, for two independent ridges of some importance leave its summit'. So, immediately after leaving the Straits, take a right fork, at a cairn. The path skirts the edge above Twopenny Crag, clearly heading round the cirque towards the clean buttress of Kidsty Pike. While still rising, however, it passes through a little group of spiky rocks and here the main path is left for a much fainter one rising to the NNE. In about two hundred yards, two cairns are reached, each competing for the honour of being the highest on Rampsgill Head; the most northerly gives much the better view down Rampsgill Beck and into the Martindale Deer Forest. Make the most of the view from here; you won't get any closer without trespassing (see below).

From Rampsgill Head the continuation of the walk is to The Knott, which AW describes as 'a protuberance that takes the shape of a small conical hill' on the steep slope descending to Hayeswater. Appropriately, there is no path from the indistinct top of Rampsgill Head to the oddity of The Knott, but the obvious path beside the wall from the Straits of Riggindale is soon reached and a very brief climb beside the wall, up the short side of the fell, leads to the top. From here, the crags on Rampsgill Head, unseen from the summit, come clearly into view, as does the continuation of the ridge rising to Rest Dodd, and AW suggests that this is now the way to go.

The crumbling wall from The Knott leads down to a depression and then climbs back almost to the summit of Rest Dodd. If you traverse its summit, you may be technically trespassing and the Martindale Estate do not encourage any right to roam, although there are no signs to make clear the boundary of the (mostly treeless) deer forest. AW says there are three cairns there and an eroded peat-hag and I bet the peat-hag is still there. Seen from a distance, there is no sign of the flagpole poking out of one of the cairns which is illustrated in AW's drawing. There is, however, a right-of-way path, curving round the base of The Knott and then traversing across the flank of Rest Dodd. This path leads off steeply down a slope of grass and peat-hags to a junction where a sharp left turn heads downhill for Hayeswater. From this junction, ensure you continue contouring to the north-west across the slope; the path occasionally seems to vanish in bog and wet ground, crosses several little becks and more peat-hags but always keeps above any walls or fences that are in good repair. It finally reaches a little hause where several pools are trapped. Immediately beyond are the grey rocks at the top of Satura Crag, from where there is a good view down Bannerdale to more of the private deer forest.

Continuing along the ridge and beyond a gate at a wall-corner, Angle Tarn, with its two little islands, shortly appears. Although its south end is currently almost choked with weed, it is a delightful sheet of water, retained by a steep little crag and with distant views beyond to Fairfield and Helvellyn. The two rocky Angletarn Pikes are north of the tarn, although only one is visible from this approach, and the obvious path leads round and just above the level of the tarn towards them. On the way, it forks and the higher path leads easily to a point just below the nearest Pike from where an easy scramble soon leads to its top. It is a superb viewpoint, at the centre of an almost complete circle of fells. The other Pike, the more northerly, is about 200 yards away as the crow flies and 500 away for wingless humans and is reached by another easy scramble after crossing a boggy depression. This is the higher of the two and its status is marked by a collection of mostly tiny stones, a Lilliputian cairn.

Grass and scree lead off downhill towards Ullswater and the higher path is soon joined again, shortly connecting with the lower one at a point where there is a good view to Red Screes beyond Brothers Water. This leads down a shallow gill to reach Boredale Hause, a major junction from which paths lead over Place Fell, down Boredale and down to Patterdale. Turn down towards Patterdale but just beyond what looks like a large sheep-fold (and was the 'Chapel in the Hause' named on older maps) the path splits and you need to take the left fork leading across the beck. Follow a slanting track which crosses the fellside below the Angletarn Pikes, with good views ahead once again to Hartsop Dodd.

At a footbridge over Angletarn Beck, with a gate at the entrance to a walled lane directly ahead, cross but turn left and up beside the beck for 100 yards to a ladder-stile over the wall on the right. A delightful path now leads through woodland to pass the house of Grey Rigg by a gate and stile. Turn left along the driveway and follow it round to where it curves back into Hartsop village and the end of a splendid round.

Hartsop Dodd seen from the descent from Boredale Hause.

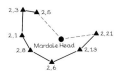

15 THE HEAD OF HAWESWATER

BEST MAP: *OS 1:25 000 Outdoor Leisure 5, North Eastern area*
APPROXIMATE TIME: *7 hours*
TERRAIN: *Grass, then peaty ground, followed by firm paths for the rest of the walk.*

ITINERARY	Book & Fell No	Height of ascent	Distance	Cumulative distance	Height above sea level	
		feet	miles	miles	feet	mtrs
MARDALE HEAD					850	259
Selside Pike	2.21	1350	3.00	3.00	2142	656
Branstree	2.13	450	1.50	4.50	2333	713
Harter Fell	2.06	700	2.00	6.50	2539	778
Mardale Ill Bell	2.08	450	1.00	7.50	2496	761
High Street	2.01	400	0.80	8.30	2718	828
Rampsgill Head	2.03	250	1.25	9.55	2581	792
Kidsty Pike	2.05	35	0.33	9.88	2560	780
MARDALE HEAD			3.00	12.88	850	259
Totals of heights and distances		3635	12.88			

Few walkers consider including Selside Pike, or Branstree, in a circuit of the fells at the head of Haweswater, and I did not either until I studied the AW ridge-line map, when it became clear that these two fells extend an already marvellous walk.

AW started up Selside Pike from Swindale, the next valley to the east, but this circuit is obviously much more easily begun from the Mardale side. The usual start for almost all walks in this area is the car park at Mardale Head where the road up the east side of Haweswater ends (grid ref 469107). But then head in the opposite direction to everybody else (don't wonder 'Why am I doing this?' *You* know something they don't), either back along the road, or on the footpath along Haweswater's shoreline, to the point where the Old Corpse Road (public bridleway sign, grid ref 479118) starts its climb up the fellside to Swindale. (It is also possible to park three or four cars on the verge here, but then you'll have the bit of road-walking at the end.)

Steep zigzags up the fellside beside Rowantreethwaite Beck lead past one ruin and to another a little higher up (probably used as resting places for corpses), providing a good

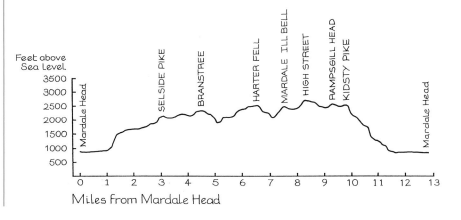

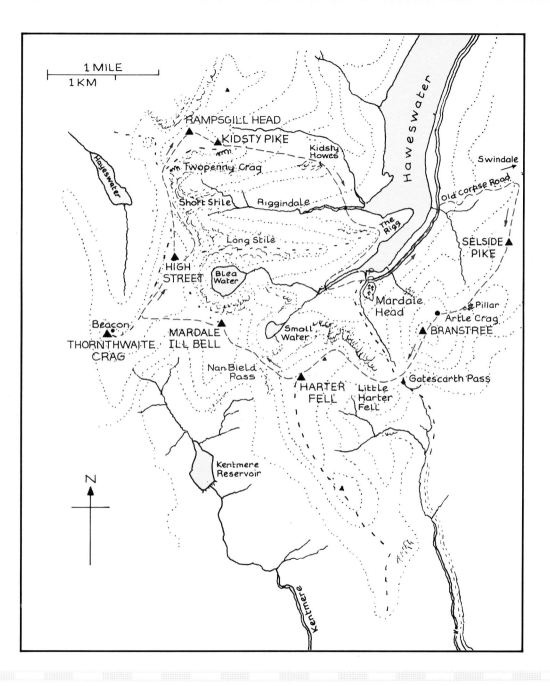

1 MILE
1 KM

Haweswater

RAMPSGILL HEAD
KIDSTY PIKE
Kidsty Howes
Twopenny Crag
Short Stile
Riggindale
Long Stile
The Rigg

Haweswater

Swindale
Old Corpse Road

SELSIDE PIKE

HIGH STREET
Blea Water

Mardale Head

Pillar
Artle Crag
BRANSTREE

Beacon
THORNTHWAITE CRAG
MARDALE ILL BELL
Small Water

Nan Bield Pass
HARTER FELL
Little Harter Fell
Gatescarth Pass

Kentmere Reservoir

N

Kentmere

The survey pillar between Selside Pike and Branstree.

excuse to pause for excellent views over Haweswater and a prospect of almost all of the day's walk ahead. Continuing, the angle gradually eases and the track, marked by cairns, reaches its high point on this broad ridge, with a view down the far side to Swindale. Here the serious work begins with a climb up grassy slopes to the south to Selside End, continuing up broad slopes to the south-west to reach a large cairn on Selside Pike. The scenic views are, sadly, not inspiring.

A wire fence rises from Swindale to the summit of Selside Pike, where it changes direction towards Branstree and this shows you the way to go. You will, however, get your boots full of ooze if you stick with the traces of path alongside it as it leads across the peat groughs called Captain Whelter Bog. I'm afraid it is a dull plod until the survey pillar, connected with the Haweswater aqueduct carrying water to Manchester, comes into sight to add some interest.

This pillar is of the same pattern as others found along the eastern watershed of Longsleddale (*see* Walk 10), built of stone and with a deep 'nick' in its top. From ground level it is not possible to see any other pillars, although Haweswater is in sight, but it is built just below the highest land and if a viewpoint level with its top is taken (you don't need to climb up it) the pillar on Tarn Crag, Longsleddale, then does come into sight. About sixty yards away are a couple of small tarns in the depression. Visible from the pillar and higher up a grassy slope is a tall, substantial cairn amongst a few flat stones but with no sign of a crag, on what AW called Artlecrag Pike but which the OS later truncated to Artle Crag. This is the next objective but it is not the summit of Branstree; this is found to the south-west, marked by an OS concrete circle in the ground and a tiny cairn. A substantial wall end 50 paces away to the south-east is much more prominent and the fence (the continuation from Selside Pike) descends from here to the south-west and will guide you down the grass slopes towards Gatescarth Pass. The shadowed rocks below Little Harter Fell and the steep black slopes and gullies on the north face of Harter Fell itself come into view on this descent.

Having picked a way across the bogs on the hause, an obvious path rises up grassy slopes, cutting a corner and avoiding the boundary stone on Adam Seat. It climbs above a first steep belt of crags falling away on the right below Little Harter Fell, and the first good view of Haweswater far below is seen from here. The path then runs alongside the now substantial fence on the next gradual rise to where the fence turns a corner. Here is another boundary stone with a letter H chiselled in it and a little cluster of boulders on the promontory above the highest crags. This is the traditional viewpoint for Haweswater, but it is also the best point for a sight of the great bulk of High Street falling to the wild combe of Blea Water below its east face.

Continuing to the south-west up the edge of the steep drop, a gradual slope leads past more cairns with rusty iron fence-posts sprouting from them to a single one, likewise embellished, on the top of Harter Fell. North-west from here is the splendid

Nan Bield Pass, almost Alpine in its situation, linking Harter Fell to Mardale Ill Bell, and a line of cairns down a stone-studded grass slope makes for the ridge leading to it. A fairly steep rocky section, with a view to Small Water below, leads over a more level top with a big sweep of crags down on the right, down another sharper descent and a final easier slope to the Pass. There is a shelter in the nick of the hause itself, a windbreak against south-westerlies; it is constructed as a stone wall with two rudimentary arms pointing towards Haweswater. I seem to remember that this was once roofed, but perhaps that is just a trick of memory.

Going round the left side of an outcrop, the path now rises up rougher ground on the far side of the pass to the north-west and towards Mardale Ill Bell. As it does, so a point is reached from where there is a view of Small Water and Haweswater directly in line one above the other, although in latter years the effect seems to have been lost as the water level has been so low. The path rises gradually across the slope, which becomes stony so that the path is not very obvious in places. In mist it can be indistinct but some little outcrops of upright, square columnar rocks are reached just before the summit cairn. On this approach from Nan Bield Pass, it is not an obvious summit, being more a gentle rising of land, but there are some small crags to the north, and then steep slopes falling towards Haweswater.

The huge flattened dome of High Street is to the north-west and there is a wall traversing its entire crest, with the trig point on the highest ground so in bad visibility a walk along a compass bearing to the north-west is bound to intersect with the wall. A turn upslope beside it will then reach the trig. In clear weather you can simply walk towards it, across a peaty depression and then curve round the edge of the escarpment overlooking Blea Water. There is a dramatic view from near the top of the gill that cuts through Blea Water Crag (which is used by a testing scramble route) and then a plod, with traces of a path, trending leftwards up grass slopes, leads to the wall along the top and the trig.

From here, in good visibility, you really should go 100 yards or so east of the trig and then walk north along the edge of the great eastern combes of High Street, steering above the top of the fine ridge which descends Long Stile towards Haweswater, and continuing above steep slopes to where another blunt ridge, Short Stile, thrusts into Riggindale. The disintegrating wall on the left will now be very close and a path beside it leads down to the narrowest part of the High Street ridge at the Straits of Riggindale, where the other path over High Street, the one following the course of the old Roman road, is joined. A short rise, and I emphasise short, up the slope beyond leads to a cairn, from where a lesser path turns off to the right, north-east, to pass above the broken buttresses of Twopenny Crag. (Whenever I see this crag it triggers a memory of an old friend looking at a new climbing guide to a small and scrappy crag somewhere: 'Three bob for the guide book! I wouldn't give yer tuppence for t'crag!'

Looking back to Selside Pike from the handsome cairn on Artle Crag.

Overlooking Blea Water from near Mardale Ill Bell.

You could be forgiven for thinking that Kidsty Pike is the next top of the day, but it is not so. AW rightly pointed out that Rampsgill Head is the next top along the ridge from High Street and important because 'two independent ridges of some importance leave its summit'. Fortunately to visit it involves just a slight deviation from the obvious path around the rim of Riggindale. This path, while still rising slightly, passes through a scattering of sharp-edged boulders and here you should turn off left (NNE) on a much fainter path. In about 200 yards the first of the two cairns on Rampsgill Head's summit will be reached. The second, the northern one, gives the best views down into the almost treeless Martindale Deer Forest.

The sharp edge formed by the summit buttress of Kidsty Pike jutting into Riggindale is unmistakable and clearly distinguishable from many directions, even from the M6 motorway. It is only a third of a mile away and to reach it involves a simple walk to the south-east across a very slight depression, joining the path around the rim of Riggindale on its last very short rise to the cairn on the solid rock buttress at the top of the Pike. Perhaps surprisingly, Ill Bell, recognisable by its shape and summit cairns, can just be seen beyond High Street's shadowed east face while afternoon light sparkles on the little tarn on Caspel Gate, seen across Riggindale.

A path now leads down straightforward grassy slopes towards Haweswater until the descent is halted abruptly at a depression. On the far side of this rises Kidsty Howes, an upthrust of rock and grass, like a breaking wave, so that you either scrabble down some rock grooves on the left side, or swing more widely left and continue down grass. Approaching the valley, swampy ground is best avoided by trending nearer to Randale Beck on the left, then an obvious footpath leads to the footbridge over Riggindale Beck. From here an easy walk, between two lines of upright flat-faced stones resembling little gravestones, goes through a small clump of larch trees and rises gradually across sheep pasture to The Rigg, the conifer-crowned headland thrusting defiantly into Haweswater. The route keeps outside the plantation wall, then curves round on a good but stony path along the west bank to cross Mardale Beck by a footbridge and return directly to Mardale Head and the car park.

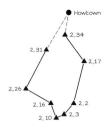

16 THE MARTINDALE HORSESHOE

BEST MAP: *OS 1:25 000 Outdoor Leisure 5, North Eastern area*
APPROXIMATE TIME: *6½–7 hours*
TERRAIN: *A firm grass and rock ascent ridge, then easy walking over peaty ground for almost the whole of the remainder.*

ITINERARY	Book & Fell No	Height of ascent	Distance	Cumulative distance	Height above sea level	
		feet	miles	miles	feet	mtrs
Howtown					600	183
Steel Knotts	2.34	900	1.00	1.00	1414	432
Wether Hill	2.17	1100	1.50	2.50	2210	674
High Raise	2.02	500	2.25	4.75	2634	802
Rampsgill Head	2.03	140	0.75	5.50	2581	792
The Knott	2.10	65	0.33	5.83	2423	739
Rest Dodd	2.16	360	0.75	6.58	2278	696
Angletarn Pikes	2.26	300	1.75	8.33	1857	565
Beda Fell	2.31	300	2.00	10.33	1664	509
Howtown				3.25	13.58	600	183
Totals of heights and distances		3665	13.58			

Of the Martindale fells to the east of Ullswater, AW preferred to treat Place Fell as an outlier, not properly part of the ridge system, so this is a round of the high land enclosing Rampsgill Beck and Bannerdale Beck. The upper valleys themselves, with The Nab between them, are the main section of the Martindale Deer Forest, a sanctuary for red deer; although the whole area may well once have been heavily afforested, there are few signs of that now. AW says that '"Keep out" notices, barricaded gates and miles of barbed wire must convey the impression that there is no welcome here'. I did not find any such obstructions when I was working on my book *On Lower Lakeland Fells* and walked out over The Nab, but the resultant problems with the Dalemain Estate, after the first edition of the book, made it very clear that it is only in dire emergencies that it may be permissible to come down the upper part of these valleys. However, this walk is not into but around the Forest, an enticing look into the forbidden land, not a trespass over it.

Start from Howtown, parking near the public launching site (grid ref 444199) or further south beyond the cattle-grid after which the road is unenclosed. From the

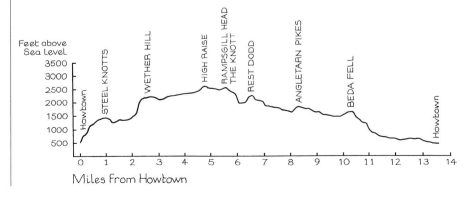

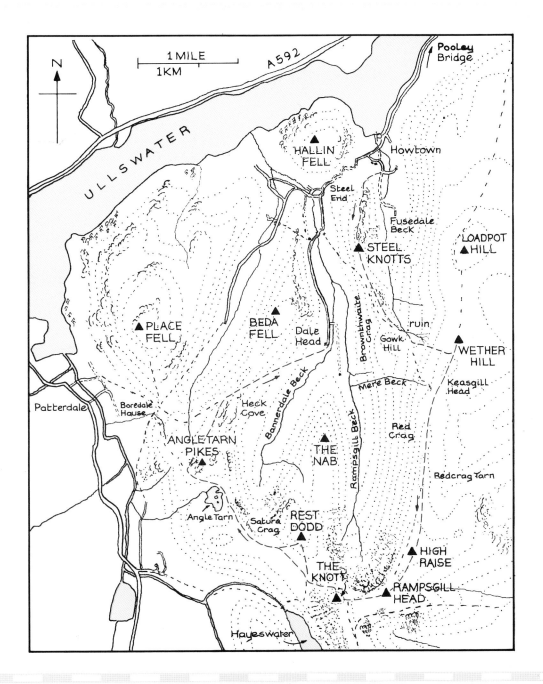

N

1 MILE
1KM

A592

ULLSWATER

Pooley
Bridge

HALLIN
FELL

Howtown

Steel
End

Fusedale
Beck

LOADPOT
HILL

STEEL
KNOTTS

ruin

Brownthwaite Crag

Gowk.
Hill

WETHER
HILL

PLACE
FELL

BEDA
FELL

Dale
Head

Bannerdale Beck

Mere Beck

Keasgill
Head

Patterdale

Boredale
Hause

Heck
Cove

Red
Crag

ANGLE TARN
PIKES

THE
NAB

Rampsgill Beck

Redcrag Tarn

Angle Tarn

Satura
Crag

REST
DODD

THE
KNOTT

HIGH
RAISE

RAMPSGILL
HEAD

Hayeswater

Looking back down the Steel Knotts ridge from the path to Keasgill Head.

launching site, walk south a short way to where the road crosses Fusedale Beck. Immediately over the bridge turn left through a gate between two trees and along the public bridleway beside the beck towards the houses and the Howtown Hotel. Reaching tarmac again, turn left and follow the road uphill to where it forks, keeping right for Cote Farm and as far as a cattle-grid at the end of the secret valley of Fusedale. Here there is a finger-post sign 'public bridleway Martindale' and a grass track quickly leads to the right to Steel End, the foot of the fine ridge leading up to Steel Knotts. A faint path climbs the ridge, with Place Fell, Hallin Fell and then Beda Fell appearing, as height is gained to reach a first cairn. An almost level stretch follows along the knobbly ridge to reach the delightful spiky top of the Steel Knotts ridge, named Pikeawassa, which is a natural place to rest a moment or two.

Go easily down on grass to a hause crossed by a wall rising from Rampsgill Beck, to meet a path rising from Martindale Old Church. You may join this path, of course, but only by deserting the strict top of the ridge. So follow the wall instead over the rise of Brownthwaite Crag before rejoining the path at a second hause and following it round a shoulder of Gowk Hill to a ruined stone hut at the head of Fusedale Beck.

Wether Hill, south-east of the head of Fusedale, is the next objective but the easiest and most obvious path, which slants up a grassy shelf across the fellside to a shallow gully at the head of Mere Beck, joins the old Roman road half a mile *beyond* the top. So, to avoid back-tracking, just make up your mind to tackle the slope direct; when you are determined, it is never as bad as you first thought. Strike up the right-hand edge of the fan of shallow gills draining the steep grass slopes above the ruined hut and a grass groove

slanting bottom right to top left will be reached. This leads onto Wether Hill, reaching the High Street path between its two tops. Here go left (north) a short way to the one with the cairn, which is apparently accepted as the main top, or right to the featureless mound which I still think is the higher.

There should be no problems with the route once the High Street path is gained as it leads south now to the depression near Keasgill Head, where the path from Mere Beck also arrives. Now the way runs between a wire fence on the right and a collapsing wall on the left, although the wall is often out of sight, on a gradual ascent up the peaty rise

Looking south from Pikeawassa (Steel Knotts) to High Raise, The Nab and Rampsgill Head.

Rampsgill Beck from Rampsgill Head, with the ridge to High Raise.

of Red Crag. The shallow depression beyond holds Redcrag Tarn, to the left of the path, then the old wall and fence slowly converge on the long rise towards High Raise seen ahead, until they turn downhill to Rampsgill Beck. The High Street path completes the climb to High Raise, although you will have to divert slightly to visit the stone-capped top with its windbreak and obvious cairn. Rejoin the path for the descent to the hause beyond but then spurn the main path (which turns south) and keep as close as safety allows to the edge of the steep and rocky ground falling to Ramps Gill on the right, to attain the stony top of Rampsgill Head, where there are two cairns.

There is little sign of a path from here (rather disconcerting in mist in such a well-trodden area) down a stony slope westwards towards the prominent little hump of The Knott, but you will intersect with the main path from High Street to Patterdale and can then turn north (right). This good path turns The Knott on its north side and you can easily make a very short diversion to its top before rejoining the path downhill to the north-west. Rest Dodd, which you will have seen from High Raise or Rampsgill Head, now lies ahead as the next top along the ridge and a broken wall crawls up the slope towards it. Unfortunately, the wall doesn't quite reach the top where, AW tells us, there are three cairns and a peat-hag, not to mention a flagpole. The top is just inside the Martindale Deer Forest and traversing its summit may be technically trespassing, although there is no apparent indication on the ground of this; most walkers obviously prefer the easier path which traverses the peaty slopes of its south-west flank. On the traverse, after some uncertainties caused by boggy bits, you will find yourself shadowing a fence and wall to a little hause where numerous small pools are trapped. Here you have reached the rim of Bannerdale and there is a good view from Satura Crag into deer country, then a good path continues, beyond a gate in a wall corner, to where the attractive Angle Tarn with its unusual notched shoreline comes into view.

Only one of the two Angletarn Pikes is visible from the path around the tarn but its rough and rocky height is unmistakable on the north side and you will reach it most easily by following the higher of two paths round the base and then scrambling to the top. The second and higher summit will then be seen across a little depression to the north and its superior status confirmed by the tiny cairn on top. From the north top, head north-east to pick up a faint trod over rough ground to reach the rim of Bannerdale again, above Heck Cove. The line of the ridge now trends slightly downhill towards a large cairn and immediately beyond it intersects with the main path from Boredale Hause to Dale Head Farm in Bannerdale.

The line of the ridge clearly continues over Beda Fell and Beda Head, then underneath Winter Crag to join the public right-of-way which runs between the farms of Garth Heads and Winter Crag. This is the way AW went and we have acknowledged this by including Beda Fell on the gradient diagram and in the little diagrammatic map. However, there is no permissive path down this ridge – I passionately wish there were.

The only alternative is to follow the path already mentioned to Dale Head Farm, and this is the red-pecked route included on my main map. You can now complete the walk down the valley; it is simple and straightforward and ends a fine round.

17 THE FUSEDALE SKYLINE

BEST MAP: *OS 1:25 000 Outdoor Leisure 5, North Eastern area*
APPROXIMATE TIME: *4 hours*
TERRAIN: *A rock/grass ridge, a grass groove and extensive peaty ground giving easy walking lead to a steep descent on grass.*

ITINERARY	Book & Fell No	Height of ascent	Distance	Cumulative distance	Height above sea level	
		feet	miles	miles	feet	mtrs
Howtown					600	183
Steel Knotts	2.34	900	1.00	1.00	1414	432
Wether Hill	2.17	1100	1.50	2.50	2210	674
Loadpot Hill	2.18	180	1.00	3.50	2201	671
Bonscale Pike	2.29	50	1.50	5.00	1718	524
Howtown			1.25	6.25	600	183
Totals of heights and distances		2230	6.25			

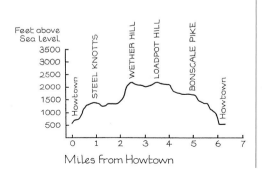

What makes the hidden valley of Fusedale so interesting to the fellwalker is its enclosing western ridge. A blunt and craggy nose overlooking Ullswater allows a delightful ascent, then its spine leads to one of the neatest rock summits in the Lakes. It is a splendid beginning to a circuit whose middle section is not very inspiring on a gloomy day although the finish is good.

The start is Howtown and it is possible to park a few cars by the jetty/public launching site (grid ref 444199). Alternative parking may be found further south along the road where it is unenclosed. From here, directly ahead due south, the rocky ridge of Steel Knotts rises in full view. Reach it by walking south along the road for about 150 yards to the far side of the bridge where it crosses Fusedale Beck, then turn left here through a gate between two trees and along the public bridleway beside the beck towards a group of houses and the Howtown Hotel. Swing left on reaching the tarmac road ahead and follow it slightly uphill to where it forks, keeping right (signed for Cote Farm) to shortly reach a cattle-grid where there is a finger-post with several signs, one being 'public bridleway Martindale'. A grassy track turns right here, just outside the intake wall, and quickly reaches Steel End, the foot of the Steel Knotts ridge. The waterworks post is still here, as AW described it, but its notice has disappeared.

Turn up the ridge here; you'll be able to follow an attractive route up the ridge, which has a few rocky steps but is mostly on grass between the outcrops, to reach a first main cairn at the northern end of the ridge where it levels off. Easier ground now soon leads to the splendid spiky top of Steel Knotts, called Pikeawassa. On the way, all the fells around the Martindale skyline come into view, with Rest Dodd and The Nab looking particularly shapely. You will be able to admire them while rummaging in your rucksack for that old Mars Bar that has turned grey with age but which will still taste delicious.

An easy descent on grass now leads to a hause, crossed by a wall that rises from Rampsgill Beck and then continues over the substantial grassy rise of Brownthwaite Crag. Stay beside the wall on its right-hand side to pass a small cairn on the summit, before

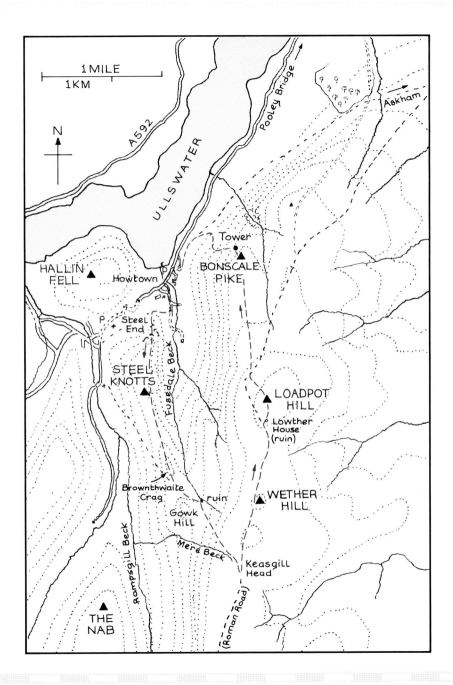

Above: The sharp top of Pikeawassa (Steel Knotts) with Loadpot Hill.

Right: The Steel Knotts ridge from Bonscale Pike:
note the red deer in the foreground.

descending to a second hause. Here a fair path (from Martindale Old Church) is joined, leading to a ruined stone hut at the head of Fusedale, where the wall turns south round the shoulder of the grassy bump of Gowk Hill.

Wether Hill, the next objective on the round, is south-east of the head of Fusedale and confusingly has two tops. The OS map shows two public paths rising up very steep grass slopes towards them, one invisible and the other only discernible with difficulty on the ground. The path that is in normal use is neither of these but leaves the ruin, heads south roughly beside the wall for a short way and then slants up a grassy shelf leading across the slope to the SSW, meeting the wall again (replaced for a short way by a fence) where it turns up a shallow gully at the head of Mere Beck. It reaches the main ridge near Keasgill Head, where it intersects with the path along the old Roman road of High Street.

Turn left now, north, and follow this over the broad and very ill-defined south top of Wether Hill, down the very slight depression beyond and up to the north top. I am not convinced that this is the higher top, but at least there is a cairn, and from beyond the next depression with its numerous peat-hags, the OS trig point on Loadpot Hill stands out like a beacon. The obvious path passes by the remains of what must have been a much more substantial landmark not so long ago when AW sketched it, but the former tall chimney of Lowther House (a shooting-lodge) is now little more than a pile of stones. The High Street path swings north-west here, going round rather than over the final slope of Loadpot Hill, but another path leads north from the ruin to the trig point and the nearby boundary stone in its pile of quartz stones.

A final top, Bonscale Pike, remains to complete the circuit and for this it is best to strike west from the trig point to intersect with the High Street again, with some grand views now over Fusedale to Place Fell and as far as Helvellyn. Follow it downhill until it swings right and contours across the north-west slope of Loadpot Hill. Just beyond the turn, a very faint trod will be seen steering along the broad, grassy subsidiary ridge for about ¾ mile towards it. When you get there you will find that there are several stone pillars, the highest built on a little crag, but there are two more a little further north. The higher one on the fellside was certainly not built by a novice but the lower was clearly built by a master craftsman and must be Bonscale Tower. After all those acres of grass and peat-hag it will be a pleasure to be here, looking out over the beauty of Ullswater again.

In order to return to the start, turn down steep grass below the tower and you will find that a grass groove cuts across the slope towards Howtown. There is a cairn at the point where it ends but you can then turn back right and down a grassy rake to lose more

Looking north from Bonscale Pike: the lower pillar is Bonscale Tower.

height. You run into a bracken zone where the paths are made by sheep – and they contour rather than descend at the gentle angle that your legs would prefer – but the level grassy Howtown–Askham path is soon reached and then a left turn leads back towards Howtown. A right turn off this at a row of cottages leads through two wicket gates and down a field to the Howtown road, directly opposite the launching site again.

18 THE ULLSWATER PIKES

BEST MAP: *OS 1:25 000 Outdoor Leisure 5, North Eastern area*
APPROXIMATE TIME: *4–4½ hours*
TERRAIN: *Excellent grassy paths lead to peaty but firm moorland and the descent (and alternative scramble-walk) are on steep grass.*

ITINERARY	Book & Fell No	Height of ascent	Distance	Cumulative distance	Height above sea level	
		feet	miles	miles	feet	mtrs
HOWTOWN					600	183
Arthur's Pike	2.28	1200	3.50	3.50	1747	532
Loadpot Hill	2.18	500	2.25	5.75	2201	671
Bonscale Pike	2.29	50	1.50	7.25	1718	524
HOWTOWN				1.25	8.50	600	183
Totals of heights and distances		1750	8.50			

This is a short circuit over the fells along the eastern side of Ullswater's northern reaches. Part of the route is a bit unexciting but the scenery alongside and over Ullswater is always delightful and this walk also has an unusual and very good scramble-walk variation to add interest.

There is a jetty and public launching site at Howtown (grid ref 444199). Nearby there is room to park a few cars; otherwise there are some laybys beside the unfenced road beyond the cattle-grid just a little further on. Opposite the jetty is a driveway and to its left is a gate and footpath signed 'Pooley Bridge and Askham' beneath a large sycamore. Go up a sloping meadow, heading towards a row of cottages on the left, then through a wicket-gate into the enclosed area but leaving it immediately by another wicket-gate on the right. A left turn now, heading north, along a very pleasant grassy level terrace, with views over Ullswater to Little Mell Fell, leads past an old barn on the left beneath a grove of old sycamores and then past a roofless barn. On the right, intimidatingly steep slopes of bracken and grass stretch up to a skyline overlooked by two stone men, one of which

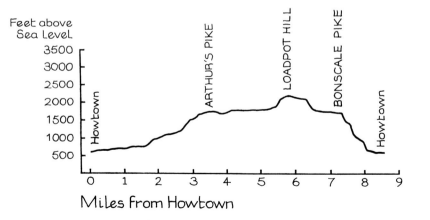

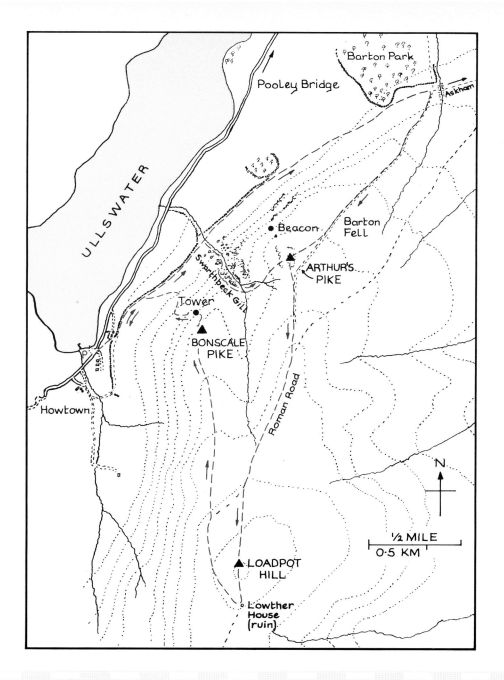

Hallin Fell seen from the lakeside path looking towards Arthur's Pike.

you will later discover is not Bonscale Tower. There are faint indications of grassy paths descending these slopes; you will be descending them on the return and they are not as bad as they look. (Going uphill, I can assure you, having returned to take photographs, they are diabolical.)

The path crosses a little stream and then the main beck tumbling down Swarthbeck Gill. AW says of this: 'Swarthbeck Gill, if it were but more accessible, would be one of the showplaces of the district.' I am afraid that such comments present irresistible temptations to me, and I even persuaded Peter Linney to accompany me, so I will shortly

A view south-west along Ullswater from the pillar on Arthur's Pike.

return to this most interesting gill. In the meantime, however, follow AW's strict injunctions to go no further than the 'ferny, tree-clad lower gorge', and then we will follow his map along the path continuing to the north-east, just outside the intake wall, for as long as it continues, and then slant upwards across the slopes below Barton Fell. At the far upper end of a plantation (Barton Park) the path reaches a junction with what looks like a grass Land Rover track and here a sharp turn back to the right is made, now heading south-west and over several grassy undulations, turning off the track to reach a higher one with a cairn, the 'summit' of Arthur's Pike. It's a very poor summit, no more than a pimple; it might just suffice in flat lands like East Anglia. Ullswater, one of the jewels of Lakeland, is not to be seen and the best view is not even of the Lake District but northwards across the Penrith gap to Cross Fell.

Fortunately, about 300 yards to the north-west, in the direction of Ullswater and on lower ground, is another cairn, but a further 100 yards below that is a large square-built beacon, about 9ft high, obviously built with care and, although crumbling a little on the up-slope side, it is far from 'collapsed' as AW saw and recorded it. It is a superb viewpoint; practically every fell in Book One is visible.

Returning to the summit cairn, a green trod across the moor rejoins the grass track, now heading south towards Loadpot Hill, a boring stretch but easy walking and the main High Street path is joined at a junction marked by a small cairn. This path is now

The upper ravine of Swarthbeck Gill.

followed, gently rising and passing a boundary stone called Lambert Lad in a groove at the side of the path, to the foot of a steeper slope. The High Street path curves round the shoulder of the fell to the right but a good trod now leads directly up to the summit of Loadpot Hill, going south. A fairly sharp rise and then a longer trudge lead to the OS trig point, No.10789, solid, square, reassuring. About 60 paces away is a boundary stone of much greater antiquity surrounded by quartz blocks, unnumbered.

Continue south on the summit path for a little way to find the remains of Lowther House, a former shooting-lodge whose stones could no doubt tell of some good carousing, but now little more than a concrete base and a few slabs of stone although I did spot a bit of glazed pottery which clearly once belonged to a loo. There is little to recall the tall chimney and fireplace illustrated by AW.

The High Street path has curved round the western slopes of Loadpot Hill to reach this same point and so you will naturally join it, making a sharp turn back to the north. The path goes gently down the slope and then turns noticeably right to contour across the north-west slope of Loadpot Hill. Shortly after the turn, watch for a faint trod turning off left along a very broad grass ridge towards Bonscale Pike. At the top of a long narrow depression, this reaches an untidy cairn that could be man-made, although the grassy mound fifty paces away looks to be higher. A hundred yards away to the north along the edge of the high ground is a more obvious cairn, built at the top of a little crag (the right-hand one seen from below at the start of the walk). A little further away and lower down and in almost direct line of sight with the beacon on Arthur's Pike is a square-built stone pillar. A path leads towards it and it then becomes clear that there are three stone structures, one above the other in line up the slope. The highest is just a jumble of stones, the middle one is the pillar already spotted, the lower is undoubtedly Bonscale Tower, another square pillar about 6ft high; this one was certainly built by an expert.

To return to the valley, just below the tower a grassy groove leads down across the slope towards Howtown and, when the groove ends at a cairn, a grassy rake turns back rightwards across the slope to continue the descent. The way becomes less obvious as it reaches the bracken zone but the slopes soon lead to the outward path just south of Swarthbeck Gill.

I promised to return to this. AW says variously that 'nervous pedestrians' should keep away from it, its upper parts are 'out of the reach of the average explorer' and 'the prudent venture no further' than the bouldery lower reaches. The first phrase is certainly true; for the rest I leave readers, or preferably walkers who don't dither on steep ground, to judge.

The lower section is very bouldery but there is a steep grassy rib on the right-hand side of the gill enabling this to be avoided. If this seems difficult, for instance during or after rain when wet grass can be treacherous, give up the idea because there is steeper

From Loadpot Hill looking west over Pikeawassa (Steel Knotts) to Ullswater.

grass ahead. At the top of the rib you can step down easily and cross the stream (which will not be possible after heavy rain) and move up into an amphitheatre above a large ash tree. The cascade ahead pours down steep moss-covered rocks choked with trees and there is obviously no way up there. However, before re-crossing the beck, look for an obvious ramp-line rising to the right from the foot of the cascade, then turning back left. Re-cross the beck and then this ramp will provide a steep but easy way, in dry conditions no more than an easy scramble, to the top of these lower falls. An upper waterfall can now be seen, falling between high, narrow walls covered in vegetation – a fine sight. Take an easier-angled brackeny slope, keeping right of the gill, to the top of the upper waterfall and you will find a little path (almost certainly made by sheep) curves into a small amphitheatre. The gill, now tamed, fades into the moor, the beck can be stepped across easily and then a slanting line over grass slopes to the north-east leads to Arthur's Pike.

I would certainly not recommend this way for a descent, but in ascent and in good conditions, it is little more than a walk up steep ground. Whilst not for 'nervous pedestrians' under any circumstances, it is certainly no harder than many routes which AW describes elsewhere without any qualifications. It provides some fine views and is a useful short cut to Arthur's Pike.

ITINERARY	Book & Fell No	Height of ascent	Distance	Cumulative distance	Height above sea level	
		feet	miles	miles	feet	mtrs
Troutbeck					850	259
Garburn Pass		900	2.25	2.25	1475	450
Yoke	2.14	850	1.75	4.00	2309	706
Ill Bell	2.09	300	0.67	4.67	2476	757
Froswick	2.12	285	0.67	5.34	2359	720
Thornthwaite Crag	2.04	480	1.00	6.34	2569	784
High Street	2.01	250	1.25	7.59	2718	828
Rampsgill Head	2.03	250	1.25	8.84	2581	792
High Raise	2.02	190	0.75	9.59	2634	802
Wether Hill	2.17	100	2.25	11.84	2210	674
Loadpot Hill	2.18	180	1.00	12.84	2201	671
Pooley Bridge			6.00	18.84	500	152
Totals of heights and distances		3785	18.84			

19 THE ROMAN RIDGE (a traverse)

BEST MAP: *OS 1:50 000 Landranger 90 Penrith, Keswick & Ambleside area. At OS 1:25 000 scale, both Outdoor Leisure 7, South Eastern area and 5, North Eastern area are needed.*
APPROXIMATE TIME: *8 hours*
TERRAIN: *Essentially easy walking underfoot, much of it over peaty ground, although quite rocky on the main ridge between Yoke and Froswick.*

When Julius Caesar landed on these shores about two thousand years ago, the Lake District was covered in dense forest almost onto the highest fells. For fast travel, the Roman legions chose the high land above the tree line which gave firmer ground underfoot and freedom from marauders and ambushes. Much of their route is traceable from their fort in the modern Ambleside to Pooley Bridge at the northern end of Ullswater and this enjoyable walk shadows it.

Considering the transport problems of this traverse, it is far better to start from Troutbeck rather than from Kentmere, leaving a car at Pooley Bridge, the end of the walk. A few cars can be parked on the side road beside the Trout Beck just off the A592 where it crosses Church Bridge (grid ref 413027). Then, although AW does not give a route from Troutbeck to Yoke, the southernmost and first top on this ridge, but goes directly to Ill Bell via Hagg Gill, the best way to Yoke from Troutbeck is by way of the Garburn Road. Reach this by turning right along the A592 from Church Bridge and

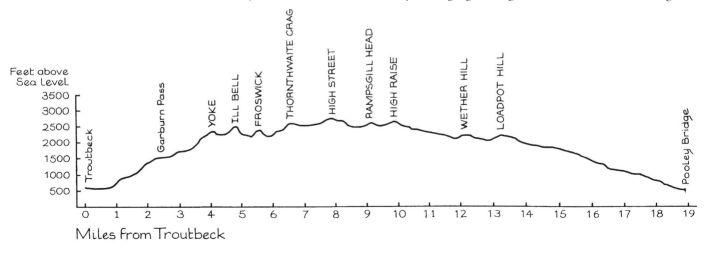

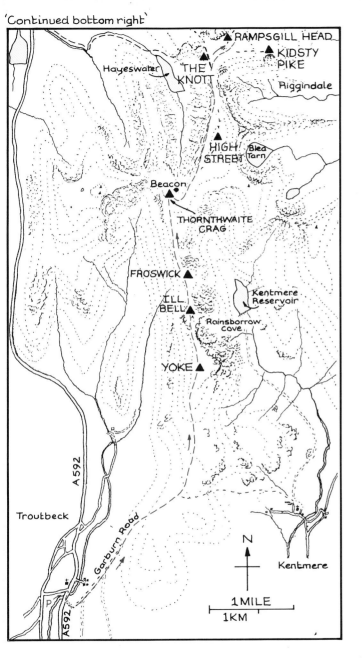

'Continued bottom right'

RAMPSGILL HEAD

KIDSTY PIKE

THE KNOTT

Hayeswater

Riggindale

HIGH STREET

Blea Tarn

Beacon

THORNTHWAITE CRAG

FROSWICK

Kentmere Reservoir

ILL BELL

Rainsborrow Cove

YOKE

A 592

Troutbeck

Garburn Road

Kentmere

P

N

1 MILE

1 KM

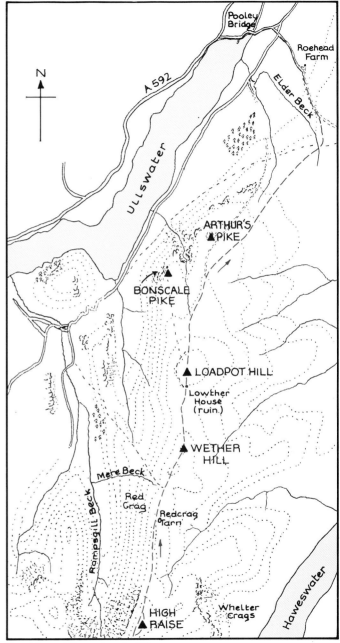

Pooley Bridge

Roehead Farm

N

A 592

Elder Beck

Ullswater

ARTHUR'S PIKE

BONSCALE PIKE

LOADPOT HILL

Lowther House (ruin.)

WETHER HILL

Mere Beck

Red Crag

Redcrag Tarn

Rampsgill Beck

Whelter Crags

HIGH RAISE

Haweswater

'Continued from top Left'

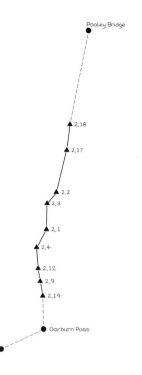

then taking the first rough lane on the left. The 'road' now winds steeply uphill, then slants more gradually across the fellside to the north-east, between walls for most of the way but still giving you good views up the Troutbeck valley, until it levels off just before the descent to Kentmere begins. The track runs out onto open fell here so take a path marked by white-topped stones across boggy ground, then along a greener level way before rising across more peaty land to reach the ridge-top wall. Veer left here to a ladder-stile further up the slope and then a firm path rises to a viewpoint cairn and finally to the main one on Yoke.

The best bit of the ridge follows as the occasional rusty iron posts of a former boundary fence mark the way along the dramatic rim of Rainsborrow Cove, followed by the climb up to Ill Bell's rocky top. That this is the reigning peak of this ridge is emphasised by three large cairns and lots of little ones. From the main one, on the highest rocks, there is a marvellous view along the continuation of the ridge to Froswick and Thornthwaite Beacon. An exhilarating switchback over Froswick is now followed by a longer rise, keeping left when the path forks at an iron straining-post with two single posts next to it. The right-hand path trends round the rim of Hall Cove towards Mardale Ill Bell, but the left-hand path, heading NNW, leads quickly to the tall stone column of Thornthwaite Beacon, above the scree and shattered rocky slope of the Crag of the same name. Four valleys are overlooked from here, with walks along all their ridges, but the Roman soldiers were not collecting tops nor looking at the views – and indeed were probably jolly lucky to get a lunch-stop – so they swung right when our route goes left to the beacon, a popular spot for a quick snack.

From the beacon, a slight descent to the east round the head of Hayeswater Gill, on a broad path swinging north-east, soon reaches the point where a collapsed transverse wall crosses the substantial one traversing the whole length of High Street. The course of the Roman road is re-joined here, now a wide track blazed across the fellside. If you too are in a hurry, you could take it as it is shorter. Because it keeps well left of the summit ridge there are some good views down to Hayeswater, but not in the same class as those from just east of the summit, reached by the other, the less used path beside the wall. This gradually climbs to High Street's trig point on a vast and almost level grassy top and you can now imagine quite easily how horses were raced here and straying sheep gathered, sorted and returned to their owners in periodic meetings of the farmers from the nearby valleys until late in the eighteenth century. Go east from the trig point (there's very little worth seeing from there unless you include orange peel and crisp wrappers) to skirt the edges of the two fine combes carved into the east face; here a wild grandeur still reigns virtually untouched by man.

Returning to the wall, or in good weather just shadowing it, continue descending to the narrow hause of the Straits of Riggindale where the Roman road merges from the left. Just a short way up the slope beyond, a cairn marks a turn uphill to the right. Up to

Froswick and Thornthwaite Crag seen from Ill Bell.

this point the main path has been more like a motorway and it is quite easy to go speeding along it towards The Knott and Angletarn Pikes without noticing the turn-off, so take care. You now need to change gear and chug up the slope on this new path to the right, north-east, soon contouring round the rim of Riggindale. Again a good path tempts you to rush off towards the sharp-edged top of Kidsty Pike seen ahead, but hold your horses: after about a quarter-mile from the turn-off and on a slight rise, the path towards Kidsty Pike passes through some spiky rocks. Leave it here, veering slightly left (NNE) and in about 200 yards the two cairns on Rampsgill Head are reached, overlooking the deep valley of the Rampsgill Beck and the out-of-bounds Martindale Deer Forest (*see* page 112), where as AW rightly remarked, 'there is neither welcome nor lodging for two-legged animals'.

Continue traversing along the edge of the high land overlooking Rampsgill Beck and you will easily pick up a path again by descending stony ground to the north-east to a depression where there is sometimes a tiny tarn and from where there is a close-up view of the crumbling crags just below the summit of Rampsgill Head. The path merges imperceptibly with the old Roman road to High Raise but by-passes that fell's top by a hundred yards to the west, so steer right-hand down a bit to find its large cairn in an area of stones. High Raise, as AW says, is 'the last fell, going north, with the characteristics of a mountain'. It could have fooled me, but he was right; it is just that we can't see the wide and crag-fringed combe below Whelter Crags to the east from the path or the top.

To the north of High Raise a gradual descent picks up the course of the Roman road again, marching easily over peaty ground and soon beside a wire fence and crumbling ridge-top wall risen from enemy territory in Ramps Gill on the left. Redcrag Tarn, a large peat-rimmed puddle on the right of the path, is passed on a shallow hause and the path then rises over Red Crag. There is another tiny puddle here, and a tiny cairn, but the 'crag' is little more than a few outcropping rocks, really only visible from forbidden Rampsgill Beck below.

After a rise beyond Red Crag, the fence and path follow the downslope to the next depression (near Keasgill Head), and here the fence turns down the line of Mere Beck towards the valley with a footpath shadowing it. Don't descend, but stay with the peaty plod on the high land which rises to Wether Hill. The path bypasses a dreary mound of peat hags and groughs which is unmarked by any cairn (but which I am certain is the highest point of Wether Hill) continuing to a second dreary mound, the north top, which does have a cairn. I don't think this cairn marks the top at all, but just marks the line of the High Street; from it, across another low depression, the trig point on top of Loadpot Hill is the next landmark.

Not so many years ago, it would not have been the trig point that caught the eye but a substantial building, the shooting-lodge of Lowther House. A path, indeed it is now the main path, diverts to allow inspection of what is now a ruin and even the large chimney and fireplace which AW illustrated are little more than a heap of stones. The main High Street track – the Roman road – curves left below the top of Loadpot Hill but a path directly up the incline from the ruins leads to the trig point and nearby boundary stone surrounded by quartz rocks.

Continuing north beyond the summit of Loadpot Hill, the footpath soon links with High Street again. Further down the slope a Land Rover track veers left towards Arthur's Pike but the main path stays on the course of the Roman road, and so long as it is borne

in mind that Pooley Bridge is at the northern tip of Ullswater, you can't go wrong. There are two left turns at the head of Elder Beck and then the track leads down past Roehead Farm and the tarmac road into Pooley Bridge.

I'll not forget doing this walk in 1976, a year of tremendous drought when there was virtually no rain for three months, and waterproofs were the last thing we thought of carrying. Two of us sweltered all day, then on the last leg into Pooley Bridge the heavens opened, the drought ended, and we arrived like drowned rats.

High Raise and Rampsgill Head seen from The Knott.

ITINERARY	Book & Fell No	Height of ascent	Distance	Cumulative distance	Height above sea level	
		feet	miles	miles	feet	mtrs
Mardale Head					850	259
High Street	2.01	2050	3.75	3.75	2718	828
Thornthwaite Crag	2.04	100	1.25	5.00	2569	784
Caudale Moor	2.07	560	1.00	6.00	2502	763
Kirkstone Pass			2.50	8.50	1500	457
Red Screes	1.14	1050	0.75	9.25	2541	776
Little Hart Crag	1.23	430	1.25	10.50	2091	637
Dove Crag	1.12	700	1.25	11.75	2603	792
Hart Crag	1.11	350	0.75	12.50	2698	822
Fairfield	1.05	330	1.00	13.50	2863	873
Seat Sandal	1.17	490	1.33	14.83	2415	736
Grasmere			3.50	18.33	200	61
Totals of heights and distances		6060	18.33			

20 MARDALE TO GRASMERE (a traverse)

Best Map: *OS 1:50 000 Landranger 90 Penrith, Keswick & Ambleside area. At 1:25 000 scale, both Outdoor Leisure 5, North Eastern area and Outdoor Leisure 7, South Eastern area are needed.*

Approximate time: *10–11 hours*

Terrain: *A real mixture of grass, rock, shale and peat; but it is essentially dry underfoot.*

This is a superb high-level traverse across the central and eastern fells and even though it is 'against the grain', its lowest point, the Kirkstone Pass, is still 1500ft above sea level. This would be an obvious escape point if needed. The start is from the car park at Mardale Head at the head of Haweswater (grid ref 469107). There is really no alternative to finding a willing driver to drop you off there.

The road to Mardale Head is along the eastern shore of Haweswater and leads into some of the most impressive scenery in the Lakes. The black crags and gullies of Harter Fell's north face overlook the car park as do the two great combes falling towards Haweswater from High Street. These two combes are like the arms of a drawn crossbow; the arrow is the superb Rough Crag/Long Stile ridge leading directly to the top of High Street, an ascent of which, as AW rightly says, forms 'the connoisseur's route up High Street'.

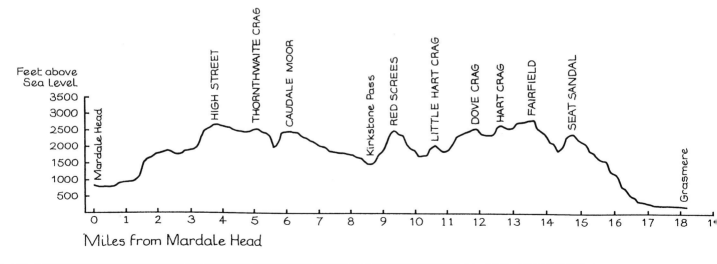

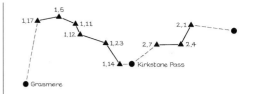

Take the footpath signed 'Bampton'. It leads to a footbridge over Mardale Beck and then a good but stony path goes along the west bank of Haweswater, just outside the larch and spruce plantation on The Rigg, then turns back sharply up the ridge. A collapsed wall runs along much of the lower part and the path runs close to its left side, below shattered crags, and you'll have grand views to Harter Fell's north face seen across Mardale. A gradual ascent follows, then there is a short easy scramble up a rock groove, followed by the traverse of the rock spine of Rough Crag. You will then descend to the hause of Caspel Gate where there is a little tarn, often dry, just to the left of the path. Another path descends from here to the outlet from Blea Water, seen below in its ice-scoured basin. Ahead rises Long Stile, a series of grass-sided but rocky tops, and you'll rise up it on an exhilarating path that finds a way across the flank of the first and then along the crests of the others, rising to reach a cairn at the top. It is all over too soon, but a backward glance to Blea Water from here is not one you will forget.

The summit of High Street is now very near and best reached by simply continuing west across the almost level plateau to reach the wall traversing its crest. Turn left when you reach it and you will get to the trig point. Its merits as a viewpoint are far inferior to those enjoyed on the ridge below, but it is the first top.

The next top is Thornthwaite Crag and a turn south beside the wall soon brings the tall stone beacon on its summit in sight ahead. The path descends gradually to the point where the remains of a short transverse wall are reached and then you can join the track along the course of the old Roman road, curving slightly right and rising up to the beacon.

Now turning north-west, the wall leads gradually and then much more steeply down-hill towards the gap of Threshthwaite Mouth, collapsing as it descends but you won't be in any doubt as to where it is heading. Loose stones and scree mean that there is a great tendency for your legs to be running faster than the rest of your body, and clapping on the anchors is easier said than done. Similar rough ground awaits on the ascent of the far slope, but going uphill, when occasional hand-touches are needed as well, will have your engines at high revs in low gear rather than in reverse thrust. Nearing the top of the slope, where the angle eases noticeably, the path trends to the south-west away from a wall corner to a large cairn which I believe marks the top of Stony Cove Pike, a good retro-spective viewpoint for High Street. The highest ground on Caudale Moor has another cairn about 200 yards away to the north-west, but you will probably neither notice it nor wish to bother seeking it.

The path from the Stony Cove Pike cairn leads south-west to a wall-corner and then through the gap there, heading west. Just beyond a rise you will spot a tarn ahead (in fact there are two tarns, although you only see one to begin with) but you will by-pass it as the path stays close to the wall traversing Caudale Moor. When the wall turns south the path does likewise, passing close by the cairn marking John Atkinson's Monument, then

On the Long Stile Ridge overlooking Blea Water to Harter Fell.

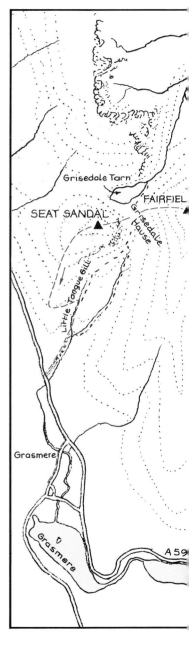

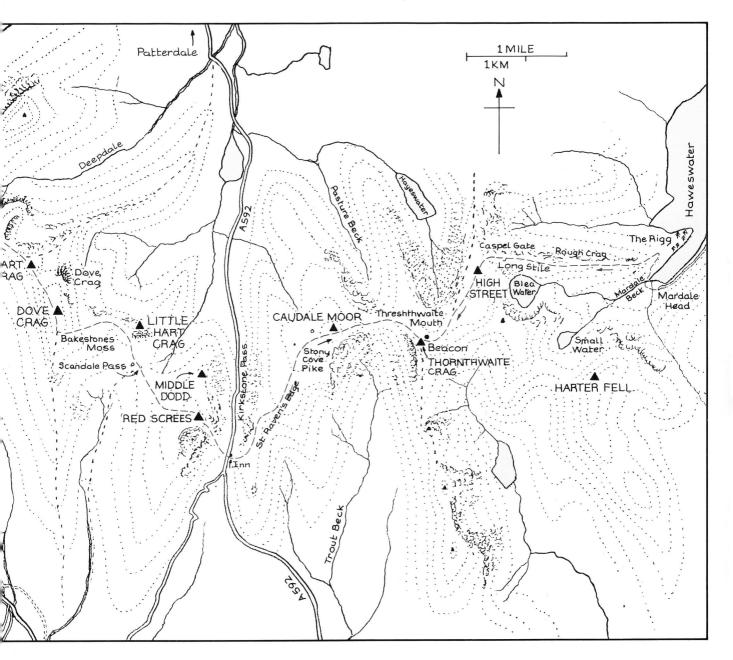

Patterdale

1 MILE
1KM

N

Deepdale

A592

Pasture Beck

Hayeswater

Haweswater

The Rigg

Caspel Gate   Rough Crag

Long Stile

Mardale Beck

DOVE CRAG

Dove Crag

LITTLE HART CRAG

CAUDALE MOOR

Threshthwaite Mouth

HIGH STREET

Blea Water

Mardale Head

DOVE CRAG

Bakestones Moss

Scandale Pass

MIDDLE DODD

Stony Cove Pike

Beacon

THORNTHWAITE CRAG

Small Water

HARTER FELL

RED SCREES

Kirkstone Pass

St Raven's Edge

Inn

Trout Beck

A592

Looking over Gray Crag to High Street from one of the cairns on Caudale Moor.

leads easily downhill to a boggy hause. A short rise follows, the path winding amongst the outcrops on St Raven's Edge as far as a large cairn. This has obviously been made from stones pinched from the nearby wall and from the gap left as a result you can get a good view down and across the Kirkstone Pass. A sharp descent follows down the slope to the Inn.

You could well be tempted to stop briefly at the pub; it will do wonders for your morale, temporarily, and the effects will be rapidly dispersed as you tackle the next stage, the rise to the top of Red Screes opposite. The path to Red Screes makes for the

Froswick and Ill Bell seen from near Stony Cove Pike.

bottom of a broad ridge defining the right-hand side of the steep south-east combe and the ascent is in zigzags over rough ground, without any particular difficulty other than that of putting one foot in front of the other. The path leads directly to the cairn, a windbreak and the trig point on the summit and it is a splendid viewpoint, particularly to Patterdale and Ullswater, but also towards Windermere and to the eastern fells just traversed.

A few more cairns lead off to the north, marking the descent down the ridge to Middle Dodd and, although this may not seem like the right way to go, after passing the first one or two another line of cairns shows the direction to take to the north-west down the slope of Red Screes towards the Scandale Pass. You will cross a collapsed wall and then be able to pick up a faint path traversing the slope towards the other wall rising from the pass and can complete the descent.

This wall continues up the far slope towards the next objective, the fine rocky double top of Little Hart Crag, but it soon turns away to encircle Scandale. However, the remains of a wire fence lead to the NNW, passing little Scandale Tarn and reaching a grassy shoulder just to the west of the crag. You can scramble easily from here to its highest top and cairn, and enjoy a good view down the length of Scandale. The line of the fence-posts now defines the rest of the climb, over some rough grass and boggy bits, onto Bakestones Moss, where it makes a turn to the west and then climbs steeper and more shaly ground to emerge onto an almost level ridge top opposite a substantial wall. Turn right here, up a gradual slope, to find the cairn on Dove Crag built on some slabs of rock just east of the wall. Continuing north-west, still beside the now tumbledown wall, it is only on the last ascent to Hart Crag that a backward glance may reveal the great cliff of Dove Crag from which the fell derives its name.

The OS map shows something called 'Priest's Hole (Cave)' here. This is well worth visiting on another occasion (you won't have time today), although it needs a head for heights as it is high above the steepest rock faces on the crag – and steepness here means overhanging. It can provide a good night's bivouac, so long as you aren't apt to sleep-walk. I spent a night here myself, together with my young son and a friend when they were about ten years old. Having promised them a hot drink, I found I had forgotten the bivvy stove, so we had to have cold water rather than a brew-up that night. The kids said I was 'a dozy prat', which is marginally better than being 'a boring old fart', I think.

Hart Crag is reached just after a short stony rise, where the wall ends, and then the walk to Link Hause is dominated by the vertical rock walls of Scrubby Crag facing you on the descent. The path rising up a slope of boulders from the hause and then curving towards Fairfield is now a broad highway, marked by cairns. Under winter conditions, when all traces of passage are buried, it can seem a fiercely inhospitable place. As you near Fairfield's stony plateau, don't just rush along: the views down the north face to Deepdale are outstanding and exhilarating, a tremendous mountainscape only challenged in quality by that at the head of Mardale.

Cairned paths lead off the top but it will pay you, even in clear conditions, to check the compass bearing if you are not familiar with the landscape. The most obvious cairned paths lead south-east (the direction from which you have just arrived) and south (for Great Rigg) but the direction needed is west, across a stonefield and then curving downhill towards Grisedale Hause.

The final top on the traverse is Seat Sandal and after the long descent it will seem only a short climb up a well-scoured slope to reach the summit cairn next to the remains

of a cross wall. The best views are undoubtedly down Grisedale, over Grisedale Tarn. The final descent is down the south ridge, an easy angled stroll on grass but with little sign of a path until the ridge sharpens and the road through the pass of Dunmail Raise can be seen below. Turn left when you reach an intake wall where there are signs directing you to Little Tongue Gill and then turn right to join a major path. This will lead to a walled lane and the A591. Grasmere is now about half a mile away to the left, and you will, incidentally, pass the friendly Traveller's Rest pub on the way. After such a long day, your throat will probably benefit from a quick gargle.

Middle Dodd seen from Red Screes.

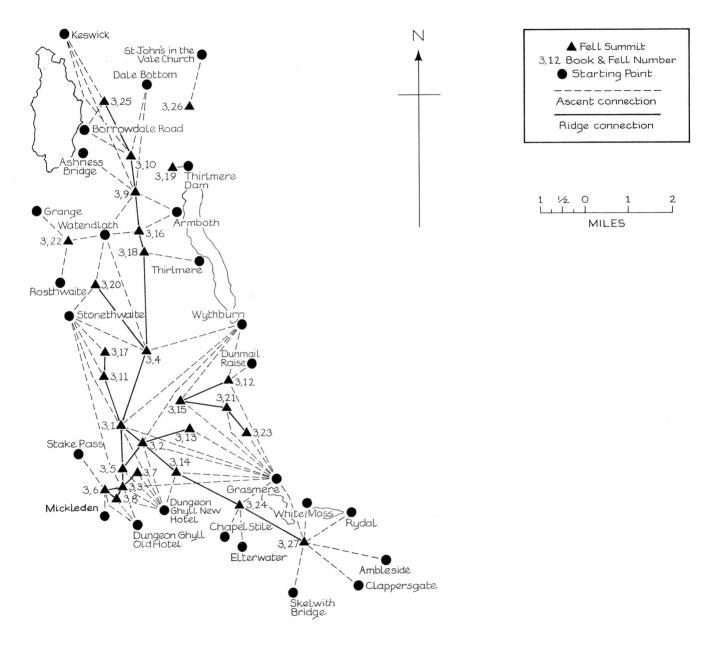

N

Fell Summit
3,12 Book & Fell Number
Starting Point
‑ ‑ ‑ ‑ ‑ Ascent connection
Ridge connection

1   ½   0   1   2
MILES

Keswick

St John's in the
Vale Church

Dale Bottom

3,25

3,26

Borrowdale Road

3,19   Thirlmere
Dam

Ashness
Bridge

3,10

3,9

Grange

Watendlath

Armboth

3,22

3,16

Rosthwaite

3,18

Thirlmere

3,20

Stonethwaite

Wythburn

3,17   3,4

Dunmail
Raise

3,11

3,12

3,15   3,21

3,1

3,23

Stake Pass

3,2   3,13

3,5

3,14

3,6   3,7

Grasmere

Mickleden   3,3

3,8   Dungeon
Ghyll New
Hotel   White Moss   Rydal

Dungeon Ghyll
Old Hotel   Chapel Stile   3,24

Elterwater   3,27   Ambleside

Clappersgate

Skelwith
Bridge

PART THREE

THE CENTRAL FELLS

21 THE GREENBURN ROUND

BEST MAP: *OS 1:50000 Landranger 90 Penrith, Keswick & Ambleside area. At 1:25000 scale, both Outdoor Leisure 7, South Eastern area and Outdoor Leisure 4, North Western area are needed.*
APPROXIMATE TIME: *4–5 hours*
TERRAIN: *A fine grassy ridge on the ascent, some boggy bits in the middle section and a broad rocky ridge with firm paths for the return.*

ITINERARY	Book & Fell No	Height of ascent	Distance	Cumulative distance	Height above sea level	
		feet	miles	miles	feet	mtrs
GRASMERE					200	61
Steel Fell	3.12	1650	3.25	3.25	1811	553
Calf Crag	3.15	300	1.50	4.75	1762	520
Gibson Knott	3.21	100	1.25	6.00	1379	420
Helm Crag	3.23	320	1.00	7.00	1299	398
GRASMERE			1.50	8.50	200	61
Totals of heights and distances		2370	8.50			

This attractive short circuit appears to be still relatively unwalked on its eastern half, although the ridge from Calf Crag to Helm Crag is frequently traversed. Perhaps it is the tarmac walk from Grasmere to begin the walk up Steel Fell that acts as a deterrent? Are we all getting soft. This is the way AW did it. To quote him precisely: 'Although this is not one of the best-known Grasmere excursions, it is a walk that all who stay here should find time to do, especially if combined with a return via Helm Crag.' Look on the bright side: there is almost no traffic, it is very difficult to park anywhere nearer so there will be almost nobody else on the walk. Thus does a disadvantage become a benefit.

Starting from Grasmere, the most convenient parking will be found up Easedale Road, which starts from the centre opposite Sam Read's bookshop and next to W. Heaton Cooper's Studio. (Alternative parking may be found on the north side of the village on the Keswick Road.) Walk north-west up Easedale Road until just beyond Goody Bridge, then turn right along the minor road below steep slopes falling from Helm Crag to reach Ghyll Foot (farm). The road, now a gravel drive, leads uphill to two

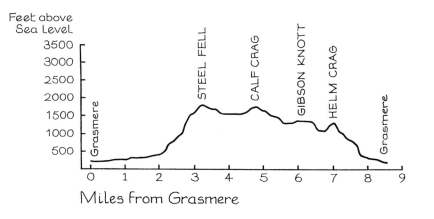

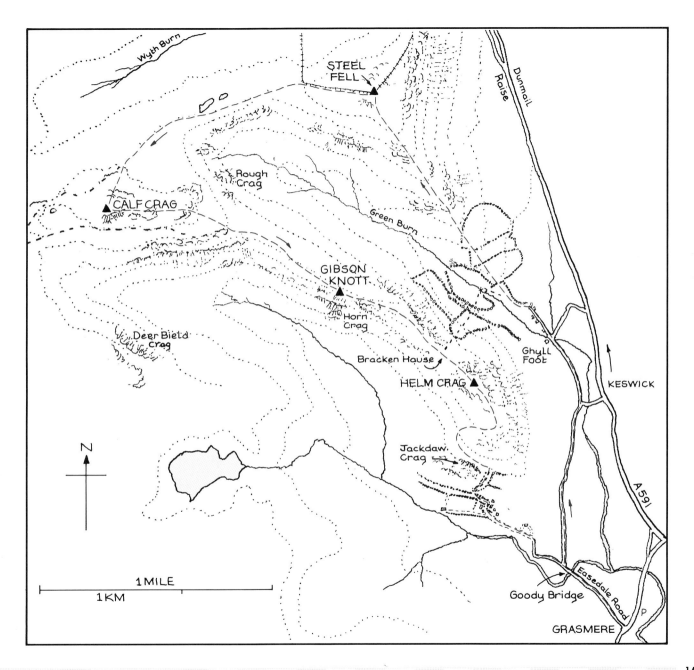

STEEL
FELL

Wyth Burn

Dunmail
Raise

Rough
Crag

CALF CRAG

Green Burn

GIBSON
KNOTT

Horn
Crag

Deer Bield
crag

Bracken House

Ghyll
Foot

HELM CRAG

KESWICK

N

Jackdaw
Crag

A591

1 MILE

1 KM

Goody Bridge

Easedale Road

P

GRASMERE

Codale Tarn seen from the ridge between Sergeant Man and Blea Rigg.

Youdell Tarn with the Langdale Pikes.

Right: Looking back towards Grasmere from Tarn Crag.

cottages at the foot of the fell. One of these, Turn How, has been here a long time: its first owner could have rejoiced at the news that the Spanish Armada had been defeated in 1588. As a gate just beyond, where there is a National Trust notice 'Green Burn', and from where a footpath leads up the valley bottom, turn sharp right instead and then an obvious grassy footpath will be seen leading through bracken and up the spine of the delightful grassy ridge to the north-west.

Beyond a gateway and a kissing-gate, the path rises gradually to a rock outcrop, skirted on the right, after which the grassy ridge continues rising to a shoulder from where the summit rocks on Helm Crag on the opposite side of the Greenburn valley take on new shapes. The 'Lion and the Lamb' are generally considered to be those at the south-east end of Helm Crag; at the north-west end are more rocks which look very much like the Lion and the Lamb from the main road near Dunmail Raise, and are called so by AW – but he also says these are known as 'The Old Woman playing the Organ'. I've heard them called 'The Howitzer' and it is that gun-like resemblance which is strongest to me when seen from this ridge leading to Steel Fell. In the opposite direction you can see beyond the drumlins in the pass of Dunmail Raise to the long western slopes of Helvellyn.

Steeper ground rises beyond this shoulder and any chatting to your companions will be reduced to gasping, while the path ascends in zigzags. Then it leads up onto a broad grassy top to some old iron fence-posts, newer wooden ones (for a fence rising from Dunmail Raise) and two cairns. This is Dead Pike, says the OS; it is certainly the highest point on Steel Fell.

The line of the newer fence marks the way now along the ridge, descending slightly, with views across Wyth Burn to the rugged fringe of Nab Crags and down to Thirlmere. When the fence turns steeply downhill to the north, the peaty path continues south-west along a line of occasional old iron fence-posts curving round the head of Green Burn, passing a couple of quite large and reedy tarns (which W. Heaton Cooper quite rightly says should be called 'Steel Fell Tarns') and then rising gradually to Calf Crag where firm rock is a pleasant change from the peaty ground previously traversed. The little cairn is built above short rock walls overlooking Far Easedale and the tumble of huge boulders below Deer Bield Crag seen opposite presents a wild scene in great contrast to the cultivated fields lower down the valley. There is also a fine view back to Steel Fell and Seat Sandal, the sort of view that makes you fume when you realise you've run out of film …

The path that now leads east towards Gibson Knott is in sight from Calf Crag and leads in a wide sweep below the unkempt slopes of Rough Crag on the left, descending and rejoining the ridge where it is narrower again. It then continues just below the broken crest on its right-hand side. For purists, the crest itself can be followed, although AW describes this alternative as 'a long succession of trivial ups and downs' which, excluding the joys of escaping to the fells, sound like most things in life. As you approach Gibson Knott you will see that its southern slope has steep juniper-covered rocks falling towards Easedale. This is Horn Crag. The path leads above it and while one fork avoids the top the other rises to what is clearly Gibson Knott although, separated by a tiny depression, there are two cairns trying to lord it over each other and disputing the top.

The path continues with some undulations and then a descent to Bracken Hause, followed by the last ascent of the circuit, an obvious climb up broken rocks to reach Helm Crag. This is a fairly level rocky ridge with a jumble of boulders falling into a depression on the Dunmail Raise side and with upthrusts of sharp rock at each end. These, dependent on your point of view will take shape, as mentioned already, as Lion and Lamb, Howitzer or whatever. They give short scrambling opportunities, although AW seems to have failed to reach the highest point himself, something I find somewhat surprising in view of where he clearly scrambled around the Langdale Pikes. He was however much interested by his explorations down on the Dunmail flank where he identified a sort of ditch and parapet. Whether you poke about down there or not yourself, the crest is a good place to stop for a short while as the prospect of the vale of Grasmere is very pleasing.

It continues so as the descent is begun towards the valley, down a few sections of slabby rock to a grassy hause. AW illustrated in the Pictorial Guide the old, direct and now very eroded route to the SSE from here, but this has been superseded by a much newer path especially created by the National Trust, a better and lovely descent which swings right (west) from this hause and then leads down grassy slopes to swing back above Jackdaw Crag and then follow steps descending steeply beside a wall. Turn right on a tree-shaded grassy track at the foot of the fell and then immediately left through an iron gate to reach the tarmac road and a cluster of attractive houses. From here the metalled track leads, on the level, directly back to Grasmere.

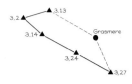

22 THE EASEDALE TARN SKYLINE

BEST MAP: *OS 1:50 000 Landranger 90 Penrith, Keswick & Ambleside area. At OS 1:25 000 scale both Outdoor Leisure 6, South Western area and Outdoor Leisure 7, South Eastern area are needed.*
APPROXIMATE TIME: *6–7 hours*
TERRAIN: *Good paths, then rougher ground with very vague paths until good paths are picked up on the long descent. Intricate route-finding near Loughrigg Fell.*

ITINERARY	Book & Fell No	Height of ascent	Distance	Cumulative distance	Height above sea level	
		feet	miles	miles	feet	mtrs
GRASMERE					200	61
Tarn Crag	3.13	1600	3.00	3.00	1801	550
Sergeant Man	3.02	700	1.25	4.25	2414	736
Blea Rigg	3.14	100	1.50	5.75	1776	541
Silver How	3.24	150	2.00	7.75	1292	395
Loughrigg Fell	3.27	850	2.50	10.25	1101	335
GRASMERE			2.25	12.50	200	61
Totals of heights and distances		3400	12.50			

This ridge walk is one which it had never occurred to me existed as such until I studied Peter Linney's map but it is certainly there on the ground, although a little more imagination than usual is occasionally needed to pursue it. It goes over some attractive but seldom-visited places with many fine views and so I hope the necessarily detailed directions for the finish of the walk will not put you off.

The start is Grasmere and any of the central car parks will be suitable from which to begin the walk. The conventional start is to walk up Easedale Road found leading from the centre of the village opposite Sam Read's bookshop and next to W. Heaton Cooper's studio, but there is a more interesting variation. For this, go north-west up the metalled lane opposite the Red Lion Hotel that leads past the house of Allan Bank and curves round to some cottages beyond them. A finger-post to the right of the last of these then signs the footpath down a field to the north-east to cross Easedale Beck on stepping-stones and reach Goody Bridge Farm. You now have to turn left onto the road, the normal route, up Easedale for a very short way until it swings right, with a gate just beyond, when you should leave it again. The footpath is now signed (for Easedale Tarn) to the north-east, crossing the Easedale Beck by a footbridge and leading across level

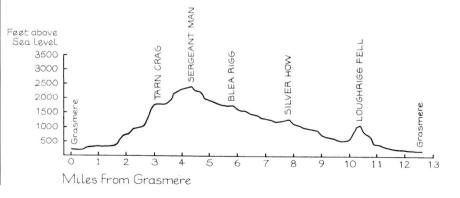

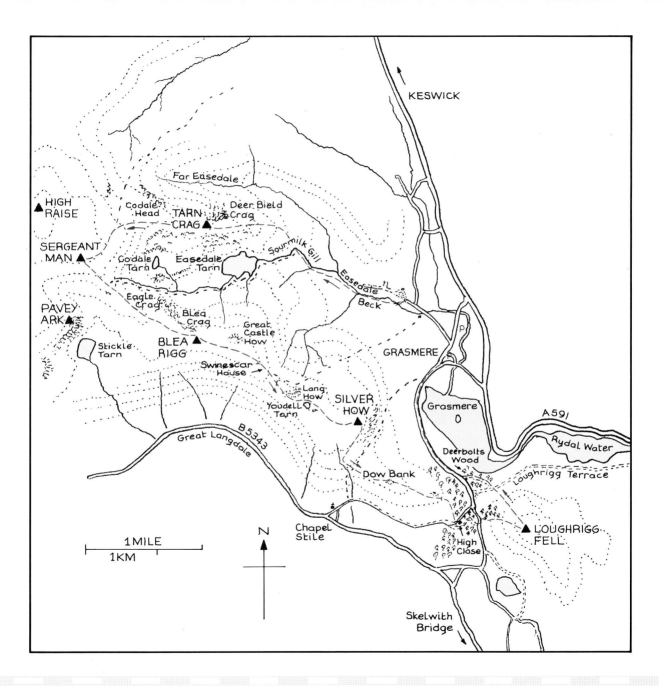

KESWICK

Far Easedale

HIGH
RAISE

Codale
Head

Deer Bield
Crag

TARN
CRAG

Sourmilk Gill

SERGEANT
MAN

Codale
Tarn

Easedale
Tarn

Easedale
Beck

GRASMERE

PAVEY
ARK

Eagle
Crag

Blea
Crag

Great
Castle
How

Stickle
Tarn

BLEA
RIGG

Swinescar
House

Grasmere

A591

Rydal Water

Lang
How

SILVER
HOW

Youdell
Tarn

Great Langdale

B5343

Deerbolts
Wood

Loughrigg Terrace

Dow Bank

1 MILE

1 KM

N

Chapel
Stile

High
Close

LOUGHRIGG
FELL

Skelwith
Bridge

On Calf Crag, looking to Steel Fell: Seat Sandal is in the background.

Horn Crag on Gibson Knott, looking along the ridge to Helm Crag.

Right: Helm Crag and Grasmere.

meadows towards the white waterfalls of Sourmilk Gill which you can see ahead. Looking beyond and just left of the falls, you should be able to pick out a small grey crag and immediately behind it, on the far side of Easedale Tarn, is Tarn Crag, the first objective.

Accompany the band of pilgrims (there is normally a steady stream of them coming up here) on the pitched path beside the gill to where it takes an obvious left turn (south-west) at the head of the falls. This is where you leave it to cross the beck on large stones (or give your feet a treat and paddle over) and follow a convenient trod to gain the base of the long broad ridge, with Tarn Crag ahead, dividing Easedale from Upper Easedale. The slope is well clothed in bracken lower down, turning toast-brown in autumn and where my little dogs disappear for minutes at a time. As you gain height, the ridge sharpens, passing an outcrop where a jutting slab of rock forms a little cave. Above this, although the path is vague in places, the natural way to go is clearly along the top edges of a series of low crags, then several undulations over rocky ground lead to a grassy col, just before and to the left of the sharp profile of Deer Bield Crag, a rock–climbers' play-ground overlooking Far Easedale. To its left and higher up you will see the rocky face of Tarn Crag, the actual peak being an elegant sharp-pointed rock to the right of the face. It looks as though it will be a tough struggle to get up there through a jumble of boulders but, in fact, an easy zigzag path leads through it, curving round the summit on its left, to reach a little rocky platform, no more than twelve paces by six, with a few stones and a cairn.

Apart from the fine view back down Easedale towards Grasmere, you should just be able to see Codale Tarn, backed by Pavey Ark and Harrison Stickle. Walk over to another cairn, about 200 yards due south, for a superb bird's-eye view of Easedale Tarn down below.

I looked down this great drop with my wife once when our son was supposed to be camping down there while doing his Duke of Edinburgh Award. We looked in vain for a tent, but then a rescue helicopter circled overhead, returning several times. My wife immediately jumped to conclusions: 'It's Jonathan! I know it. Something's wrong. Come on, we've got to get this walk done as quickly as possible!' What a flap! For half a mile her feet hardly touched the ground. It just shows, doesn't it, that getting cracking is all a matter of motivation. (Of course, the helicopter was nothing to do with Jonathan at all.)

The broad and ill–defined ridge now leads west towards Codale Head and Sergeant Man, and there is a vague path with an occasional cairn but it soon fades and you have to find your own way along an indefinite edge high above Codale Tarn. Beyond that, the best way looks to be a climb up a grassy groove cut through the surrounding bilber-ries and rocky ground alongside a little stream – easier but wetter. You will begin to wonder why you ever bothered but, as the angle eases, a couple of tiny tarns are reached, then a few rusting iron posts marking the line of the old fence boundary between

Grasmere seen from the ridge between Silver How and Loughrigg Fell.

Cumberland and Westmorland. At last, here is a reasonable path and you can turn left along it, south-west, to where it leads round an outcrop. The conical rocky top seen ahead, beyond a very overgrown little tarn, is Sergeant Man.

Take a path down the slope to the east of the cairn. It almost immediately crosses a little stream flowing from one of the high tarns, then turns south-east and downhill towards Blea Rigg. Some way down the slope is a fine inclined slab of rock, from where Stickle Tarn and Pavey Ark can be seen. This is AW's '50-foot slab' and, just to be awkward, I measured it at 60 feet at its widest point. It must have grown. A little lower down the slope flattens to a depression, and both sides of the ridge are now visible. Another cairned path leads down from here towards Codale Tarn and Easedale Tarn, but stick with the main path which continues south-east along the ridge, equally well-marked by cairns.

A gentle descent, then the crossing of an area of peat-hags follows, the path keeping just to the left of a series of slightly higher rocky outcrops, one of which overtops the others and has a cairn on its summit. This is Blea Rigg, an attractive little top, although almost nobody ever visits it, perhaps because much more dramatic views are gained looking out over Easedale from the rim of Blea Crag, a hundred yards or so to the north. From here, a glance back to Sergeant Man shows it as a tiny rock pimple beyond the dark broken rocks of Eagle Crag.

The main path now winds down between two little tarns and passes a third. Look back from here and you will see that Blea Rigg is really quite a noticeable uplift on the ridge. You will pass the rocky edge of Great Castle How, then the path winds down to a boggy depression on the ridge, Swinescar Hause, and then up again over Swinescar Pike, rounding a curve and bringing the tarns below the outcrop of Lang How into view. The largest of these, known locally as Youdell Tarn, is colonised by black-headed gulls whose raucous screeching is intended to ensure that you move along very quickly. The path skirts these on their left – there are three of them, and the third is full of isolated grass tussocks – then the main path turns north-east for Easedale. You need to leave it here, on a fainter trod to the ESE towards Silver How which you should now see as the next high point on the ridge.

There are several rounded grassy eminences on top of Silver How, but the cairn marking the summit will be found easily enough (except in mist, when it can be very confusing) with steep ground descending to a depression and scree gully on the north-east side towards Grasmere. Most ascents and descents use this way, and if it is desired to cut the walk short, this would be the best way to go now, turning left on an obvious path at the foot of the scree gully, when Grasmere is only about $\frac{3}{4}$ mile away. To complete the planned walk, which from here takes a noticeable change of direction, turn south along the continuation of the ridge, on the top edge of the lovely wooded slopes overlooking Grasmere and Rydal Water. The path shortly leads past a substantial cairn, whose white top is clearly used as a bird loo, then descends quite sharply down a wide but short gully to a junction of paths.

A sharp turn left here would lead back below Silver How to Grasmere; a right turn would lead down to Megs Gill and Chapel Stile; but the grassy path you need crosses the depression here, leads ESE and is marked by cairns. It steers just below the ridge continuing towards Loughrigg Fell, on the Grasmere side. An undulating walk follows along this broad ridge, over the flattened pyramid top of Dow Bank and then reaches a little tarn on a shelf just above a wide grassy trough. On the far side are the conifers of

Hammerscar Plantation and, just a little lower down, to the right, you should see where the tarmac road crosses over Red Bank, between Grasmere and Elterwater. You will reach the road easily by descending a steep slanting path from the tarn and then veering south-east (right) across boggy land.

As I warned at the beginning, the next section, to Loughrigg Fell, is just as complicated to describe – although easy to walk, and most delightful. Turn left along the road but slant off it almost immediately down the drive leading to the grounds of High Close Youth Hostel (National Trust sign: 'High Close open to the public'). Follow the drive which becomes a good track, leading beneath superb trees and through rhododendrons, round several bends and eventually heading north-east so that Loughrigg Fell comes into sight ahead just before the track reaches the Grasmere–Skelwith Bridge road at a gate. Turn left here but only for twenty paces or so before turning right off the road to go steeply uphill on a little path. This curves to the right outside a plantation wall and then leads over a stile; a pleasant grass trod through bracken now leads uphill with a wall on the right, climbing a shoulder of Loughrigg Fell. When the wall turns away across the fell, the path continues uphill and joins the major path rising from the Grasmere end of Loughrigg Terrace. A right turn here leads up almost immediately to the finely situated trig point, on the highest of this delightful and complex fell's three summits. Its fame as a viewpoint is surely well-known. AW himself suggests six fine ridge-walks that can be seen from here and should be done, he says, within a week. Not to mention the two others that he proposes should be done before breakfast!

Leave the summit of Loughrigg by reversing the last bit of the ascent and then following the obvious main path downhill. You will soon reach a huge collapsed cairn, the 'Grasmere Cairn', from where there is a splendid view over the lake. A steeper and rougher descent follows down some stretches of pitched path to the very end of the level walk of Loughrigg Terrace. Turn left here to a kissing-gate beyond which the paths fork. The left one returns to the road at the top of Red Bank, but the right-hand one sweeps in graceful curves through the delightful Deerbolts Wood, with glimpses over Grasmere, to reach the Red Bank road lower down at a cottage and 'National Trust Deerbolts Wood' sign.

I could suggest a route from here whereby you might walk some of the way beside the margin of Grasmere lake itself, but I suspect your energy and patience will be running out now. So just turn down the road and trundle back to Grasmere village. What a surprisingly varied and, in parts, beautiful ridge walk.

Dungeon Ghyll New Hotel

23 THE STICKLE TARN SKYLINE

BEST MAP: *OS 1:25 000 Outdoor Leisure 6, South Western area*
APPROXIMATE TIME: *4–5 hours*
TERRAIN: *Good paths to the tops (the alternative route is on perfect rock) and along them, then a pathless section leads to a steep and rather loose descent.*

ITINERARY	Book & Fell No	Height of ascent	Distance	Cumulative distance	Height above sea level	
		feet	miles	miles	feet	mtrs
DUNGEON GHYLL NEW HOTEL					300	91
Harrison Stickle	3.03	2100	1.50	1.50	2403	736
Thunacar Knott	3.05	140	0.50	2.00	2351	723
High Raise	3.01	275	1.00	3.00	2500	762
Sergeant Man	3.02	60	0.50	3.50	2414	736
Blea Rigg	3.14	100	1.50	5.00	1776	541
DUNGEON GHYLL NEW HOTEL			1.50	6.50	300	91
Totals of heights and distances		2675	6.50			

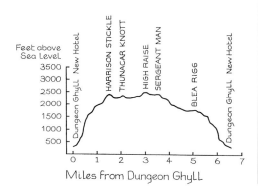

I thought I knew the Langdale Pikes area inside out and had walked, scrambled and climbed everywhere here (ground covered in my own *On High Lakeland Fells*). But not until I studied the ridge-line map produced by Peter Linney did I spot the round I describe below. It includes a direct variation on the route to Harrison Stickle of which I am certain AW would have approved, if he'd spotted it, and is a splendid day's outing.

There is a large National Trust car park, now called 'Stickle Ghyll car park' on the north side (on the right going up Great Langdale) of the B5343 next to the complex of buildings that includes the Dungeon Ghyll New Hotel and Stickle Barn (grid ref 295064). Just inside the entrance and at the end farthest from the buildings is a path signed for 'Dungeon Ghyll and Mickleden'. Take this, beneath a few trees and up a slope, and as you ascend you can hardly fail to see, directly ahead to the north-west, a shapely, pointed little rock summit. This first objective is Pike Howe – spelled How by AW. Turn left as you reach a kissing-gate, on the old track between the Old and New Dungeon Ghyll Hotels, but at the gate immediately ahead turn right, pass a bench-seat and cross a stile on the edge of the wooded Dungeon Ghyll. Do not cross the beck but follow the path rising beside the wall on the right and beneath steep rocks on the lower slopes of Pike Howe. When it forks, go left up an engineered path which rises quite steeply towards Pike Howe, with a good but distant view of the upper falls of Dungeon Ghyll ahead on the left. The path skirts the actual summit of Pike Howe by a few paces, but it is definitely worth a quick diversion to its flat-topped solid rock spike for it commands a splendid view over the Langdale valley. It is also an excellent spot from which to inspect the ridge now rising ahead to Harrison Stickle, the highest of the marvellous Langdale Pikes.

The standard path to the summit from Pike Howe, although described by AW as the 'purest' route, actually deserts the ridge leading directly to Harrison Stickle and sneaks round the back to the top. I will complete the walk using this standard route up Harrison Stickle, but will return at the end to describe an excellent and exhilarating route directly up the ridge to the top, of which I do not think AW was aware, but which is best picked out from Pike Howe.

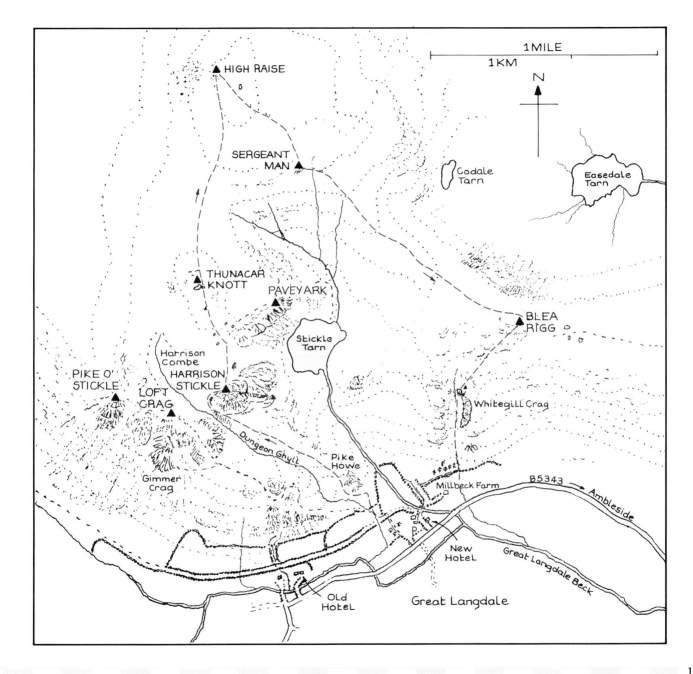

HIGH RAISE

SERGEANT MAN

Codale Tarn

Easedale Tarn

THUNACAR KNOTT

PAVEYARK

BLEA RIGG

Stickle Tarn

Harrison Combe

HARRISON STICKLE

PIKE O' STICKLE

LOFT CRAG

Whitegill Crag

Dungeon Ghyll

Pike Howe

Gimmer Crag

Millbeck Farm

B5343

Ambleside

P.

New Hotel

Great Langdale Beck

Old Hotel

Great Langdale

1 MILE

1 KM

N

Pavey Ark and Stickle Tarn seen from the top of Harrison Stickle.

The standard path leads obviously ahead up the grassy ridge which broadens as it rises, but soon also begins traversing rockier ground and making for a narrow defile where it squeezes between the rocks of Harrison Stickle and the upper part of the gorge of the Dungeon Ghyll. A slender path leads through this defile and into the high hanging valley of Harrison Combe, then curves back sharp right and climbs up a stony and rocky way to the top. It is simple, obvious and straightforward and leads rapidly to the almost flat, sickle-shaped rock summit. Apart from both a northern and a southern cairn, I recently counted at least six others. The views are outstanding, particularly down to Stickle Tarn and the great cliffs of Pavey Ark, seen from here to be out on a spur of its own.

Thunacar Knott, the next top, is little more than a swelling on the moor to the north-west, with a scattering of rocks on its summit. It is soon reached by leaving Harrison Stickle on its north side, skirting a rock outcrop on its left and passing several tiny tarns, but then just heading for the highest ground to the north-west. When you arrive, the rocks are found to be stacked up like grey roof-slates on edge. The first cairn seems to be the highest point, and according to the OS heights, is the top. But then you spot a much bigger cairn, further north beyond a small depression containing two tarns, one much smaller than the other, so doubt arises. If you are peak-bagging it might pay to touch them both. (I never used to quibble about heights and things like that; it just shows how Wainwright's little ways have got under my skin!)

On the descent to the depression towards High Raise, the most obvious feature of the landscape ahead (since High Raise is still out of sight) is the conical shape of Sergeant Man and, just beyond the lowest point in the depression, a cairn marks where a path curves out towards it. Don't turn off; the main path continues uphill over stretches of peaty ground cut by man-made drains, then levels out; ahead on the skyline is what proves to be a large two-chambered windbreak; this hides the trig point on High Raise's summit which is ten paces beyond it. The best view is almost certainly that to the north, to Skiddaw.

Previously visible, Sergeant Man is now out of sight to the south-east, hidden by the curve of the fell, but a grassy path leads in that direction, by-passing an evil-looking tarn in very peaty ground, then shadowing a line of fence-posts which come into view towards some little tarns glinting in a depression ahead. The path then veers right and over some flat slabby rocks (past a definite hollow containing a tarn on the left) and then up a short slope to the rock summit of Sergeant Man. Although blocked by the tedious slopes of High Raise to the north and west, Scafell Pike, Bowfell and Helvellyn can all be seen.

Heading on south-east towards the broad ridge separating Great Langdale from Easedale, cross a little stream, and then a well-used and cairned path leads fairly steeply down to pass the base of an easy-angled flat slab of rock (AW's 50-foot slab). The path then winds down more gently, and you will see Easedale Tarn and then the higher Codale Tarn on the left, just before the ridge runs out onto an almost flat depression. A path descends to Easedale from here but the main path undulates along the broad and potentially confusing ridge top to the south-east; it is worth making a slight diversion to the right (south) to appreciate the splendid views of Pavey Ark and Stickle Tarn. Wind round, or over, a zone of peat-hags, staying just on the left (Easedale side) of the rock outcrops along the ridge to reach Blea Rigg. It is not very obvious when you do reach it as the path passes below and to the left of the summit, but there is a cairn on its rocky top and the noticeable descent just beyond makes you realise that you are leaving a high point (it is at grid ref 302078 approximately, the OS using the name Blea Rigg to refer to the ridge rather than the top).

From its knobbly top, it can be seen that very slightly higher land does indeed curve gently to the south, towards Great Langdale. The next objective is therefore an obvious rocky high point crowned by a small cairn, reached by a trackless descent to the SSW (for those who recognise it, this direction is in line with Pike o'Blisco on the other side of the Langdale valley). When you get to the rocky point, you will find it to be directly above the steep ravine of White Gill whose left flank consists almost entirely of Whitegill Crag, a fine rock-climbers' playground (where I have spent many happy hours and some terrifying moments). The view from here, which is outstanding, is down

From the head of White Gill looking down to Great Langdale.

the rock-sided V-shaped cleft to the immediate left of a rock buttress, to the valley floor.

A descent down the continuation of the ridge above the crags is possible but I would not advise it as, apart from other difficulties, it ends in the very steep rocks of Scout Crag. The easiest way probably is to descend the easy ground into the top of White Gill, where the stream is usually unseen beneath a choke of boulders. The quickest way is also down into the bed of the gill by way of the V-shaped rock cleft; walkers blessed with large posteriors will gain additional valuable friction from the sloping rock sides. The cleft leads quickly to a junction with the well-used loose and shaly path descending the rest of the gill. It sounds and is, I'm afraid, fairly horrible but you have a great opportunity to see rock-climbers in close-up action on this superb crag, a grandstand view; this is improved even further if you are prepared to scramble onto grass slopes on the right, before resuming the descent.

The main path continues down the usually dry bed of the gill: the water does reappear for a short distance at a spring just below an ash tree, then flows underground again. A right turn when the intake wall is reached at the foot of the gill leads along the edge of a little larch plantation, the path continuing to reach a gate and kissing-gate (where there used to be a big ladder-stile). A left turn down Stickle Ghyll, on a pitched path between walls, leads to the signed path beside Millbeck Farm, over a footbridge and then into the grounds of the New Dungeon Ghyll Hotel. The way to the car park is signed and, as luck would have it, goes right past the entrance to the bar of Stickle Barn. A warning, however: when I last wanted just a pint I couldn't get one without buying a meal and I'm afraid I only just desisted from waving two fingers in a well-known salute.

I promised to return to a direct route to Harrison Stickle, best seen from Pike Howe and which will be of interest to walkers with a little scrambling experience. From Pike Howe, the upper part of Harrison Stickle consists of an obvious conical rock buttress with the summit directly above it. To the immediate right of this buttress is a wide bay with two gullies running into it and forming a letter Y. Immediately right of these two gullies – in effect the right-hand arm of the bay – is the easy-angled south-east ridge rising from bottom right to top left, and this gives the line of the route. It is most easily reached by following the standard path until nearer Harrison Stickle and then slanting up grass to the right-hand end of the wide bay where the rocks curve round and Stickle Tarn comes into view. Go just right of the last little buttress but then turn back sharp left towards the summit, up easy-angled rock covered in little knobbles and nodules and giving perfect friction. All too soon this lovely rock gives out onto tongues of grass and less continuous rock outcrops which lead rapidly to the summit. It is a delightful way up this fine peak.

24 THE PIKES AND THE ARK

BEST MAP: *OS 1:25 000 Outdoor Leisure 6, South Western area*
APPROXIMATE TIME: *3½–4 hours*
TERRAIN: *Mostly on good paths, some shaly, some rocky. The alternative scramble is on good rock and grass.*

ITINERARY	Book & Fell No	Height of ascent	Distance	Cumulative distance	Height above sea level	
		feet	miles	miles	feet	mtrs
DUNGEON GHYLL NEW HOTEL					300	91
Loft Crag	3.08	2000	1.75	1.75	2270	692
Pike o'Stickle	3.06	170	0.33	2.08	2323	709
Harrison Stickle	3.03	350	0.50	2.58	2403	736
Pavey Ark	3.07	100	0.50	3.08	2288	697
DUNGEON GHYLL NEW HOTEL			1.75	4.83	300	91
Totals of heights and distances		2620	4.83			

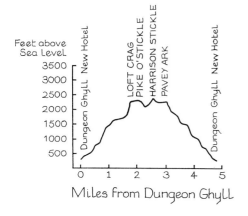

There may be some argument as to how many Langdale Pikes there are but there is very little disagreement about their superb quality. Lower than many surrounding fells, their distinctive shapes and rock architecture make them outstandingly attractive to all walkers and climbers. This ridge-line circuit links four of the possible five contenders, only Thorn Crag (which AW did not count as a 'top' but which could easily be included anyway) being omitted. It is unquestionably one of the finest rounds in the area.

The best start is from the National Trust car park on the north side of the B5343 going up Great Langdale, the 'Stickle Ghyll car park' next to the complex of buildings that includes the Dungeon Ghyll New Hotel and Stickle Barn (grid ref 295064). Leading north out of the car park and opposite the entrance is a path signed 'Dungeon Ghyll and Mickleden' and this rises beneath a few trees and then up a short slope to the north-west to reach a kissing-gate. Turn left here, on the track to the Old Dungeon Ghyll Hotel, but then go right at the gate immediately ahead and up the slope past a seat to a stile beside Dungeon Ghyll. Over the stile, turn left and ford the beck on large boulders, then an obvious path leads up beside the wall on the left. About a hundred yards after the wall ends, a fainter path branches to the right (not always obvious in summer bracken) and this leads quickly to the edge of the gill where a large boulder bridges the deep gulf below and a glimpse is obtained of the Dungeon with its cascade. Get too close and you could easily suffer a fate worse than a wetting.

Rejoin the main path which rises through bracken to a sloping wide shelf, winds round a couple of rock outcrops and reaches a large cairn where it levels off. An even traverse for a short distance leads to a point above Middlefell Buttress (the climbers' way up the fell, at the west end of Raven Crag) with a view straight down the gully beside it to Middle Fell Farm, then rises again to a broad grassy plateau, with Harrison Stickle's crags facing across the upper reaches of Dungeon Ghyll. The path now rises towards the rocks and grass ledges of Thorn Crag, to a cairn beside the ruins of a sheepfold at the base of the rocks.

From here a narrow path traverses westwards across the fellside, descending slightly,

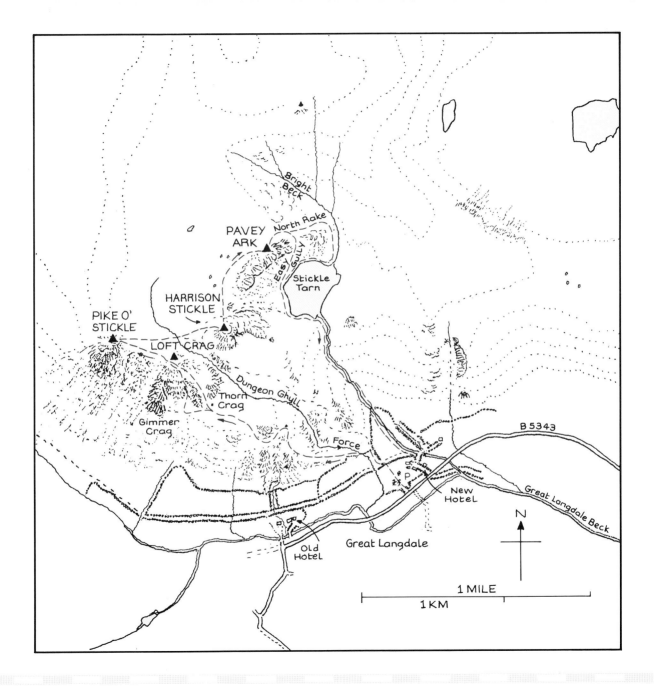

PAVEY ARK

Bright Beck

North Rake

Easy Gully

Stickle Tarn

HARRISON STICKLE

PIKE O' STICKLE

LOFT CRAG

Dungeon Ghyll

Thorn Crag

Gimmer Crag

Force

B 5343

New Hotel

Great Langdale Beck

Great Langdale

Old Hotel

N

1 MILE

1 KM

Pike o'Stickle seen from Loft Crag.

shortly to give a superb view of the south-east face of Gimmer Crag which is, AW said, 'too grand a spectacle to miss'. Walkers without scrambling experience should now return to the main path. (Experienced walkers wanting a good scramble should go to the end of this chapter for details.)

The main path continues up the scree and shifting stones of the eroded main path rising up to a depression between Thorn Crag on the right and Loft Crag on the left. There is very little difference in height between them so that you may well decide to visit Thorn Crag's top anyway and then make the short ascent up a few easy rocks to the summit of Loft Crag. Ahead is a splendid view of Pike o' Stickle and two little depressions lead to a hause immediately before reaching its superb rocky cone. A steep, bare and nasty-looking scree gully leads down towards Mickleden from this hause; AW recommended this for 'expert scree-runners' but I'm afraid that all the decent scree runs, that in the ignorance of my youth I too used to enjoy, have all been run off. Nowadays there is a National Trust notice requesting, quite rightly, that no descents be made here, so that the slopes may be preserved from further erosion.

There are several variations on the obvious easy ascent up the short north side to the top of Pike o' Stickle's almost flat top. A descent of a few paces to the south-east, to the edge of the ring of steeper crags that fringe the summit, discloses what to me is one of the finest views of all in the Lake District, that of the north-west face of Gimmer Crag, surmounted by Loft Crag, with Great Langdale's walled fields far below.

The continuation of the ridge line is strictly back to Loft Crag and then to Harrison Stickle but an obvious path cuts the corner. It leads down from Pike o' Stickle and crosses the combe, the hanging valley at the head of Dungeon Ghyll, and goes over the stream and some peaty ground which is now protected by flat stepping stones. Two obvious paths now lead up to Harrison Stickle, one a direct line, the other curving further left to a hause on the left before turning right up to the curving and almost flat summit rock platform. This is another superb eyrie. Steep rocks drop away to the south, south-east and east and make it look improbable that routes can reach the summit, as they do, by any of those directions; but then it always appears worse looking down. The superb situation enhances the terrific view down to Stickle Tarn and the great east face cliffs of Pavey Ark.

After an initial short descent, the ridge continues along the broad and rocky land towards Pavey Ark. The easiest way to descend is to the north, down a stony path which skirts a rock outcrop on its left and then weaves between several small tarns. Here occasional cairns mark the way as it swings to the ENE over bare rock and a few peat-hags, passing the point where the popular scramble route from Jack's Rake on Pavey Ark reaches easy ground.

The nearby highest point on Pavey Ark, the highest amongst numerous rocky little tops here, may or may not have a cairn. The natural place for one is in a tiny rock hollow on top of the highest bit of rock, but a cairn seems to get in the way of walkers wishing to stand on the same spot, so it is regularly knocked down. There is no difficulty, however, in good visibility, in locating the place itself. The beautiful rough grey rock hereabouts gives a good idea of the delights experienced by rock-climbers working their ways up the intricate routes on the great faces below, overlooking Stickle Tarn.

The ridge ends abruptly here and a descent to Stickle Tarn follows, taking the path leading north for about a hundred yards towards the gill of Bright Beck, crossing the remains of a wall but then veering to the right (east) and down an obvious wide and easy-angled gully between rock walls, which AW named North Rake. This continues downhill to

AW's 'awkward 10 ft chockstone pitch' in the gully below Loft Crag.

curve back right and reach as far as the edge of Stickle Tarn. On the descent, you may well spot the top of Easy Gully turning down more steeply to the right and obviously leading directly below the almost vertical east face of Pavey Ark. This is no longer easy; it is unpleasantly loose underfoot and there is an awkward boulder choke. It is better not to contribute to the erosion, or give yourself any unnecessary palpitations, so continue down North Rake until the path runs out onto easy ground, crosses Bright Beck and continues along the east bank to the dam at the outlet of the tarn. The dam was built originally to ensure a water supply to the gunpowder works situated in the grounds of what is now the Langdale Estate timeshare development.

One of the most popular paths in the Lakes now goes down the right bank, crossing to the left bank (looking down) of Stickle Ghyll. Although sadly eroded in some sections, this is nicely pitched in many places and reaches a new footbridge where the downhill slope eases. A right turn here and a continuation down the right bank of the gill, curving right at the end, quickly reaches a kissing-gate leading into the car park.

I promised to return to the alternative scramble to Loft Crag. Having traversed towards Gimmer Crag from the ruins at the foot of Thorn Crag, it will be seen that the buttresses of Gimmer are almost separated from Loft Crag by a deep, square-cut gully (South-east Gully). This is used as a rock-climber's descent and could be used by an agile and confident walker (although I emphasise the adjectives) as a means of ascent. But it does involve much hand and foot work, and at a rather exposed point an awkward step has to be made to the left from one branch of the gully to another. If you are not *certain* of your ability, do not consider it.

However, to the right can be seen a broad mass of steep rock buttresses with some grassy ledges, leading round into a wide depression which narrows to a short gully at its left-hand side. As can be seen from below, this gully is blocked by a chockstone at its top and a line of pocket-steps leads up the lower part of the depression to the gully to reach it. Here is AW's 'awkward 10ft chockstone pitch'. A short person will find it at least awkward and maybe impossible. I am frankly surprised that AW, a most careful and cautious person, but also, as he says, 'over six foot tall and fourteen stone in weight' got up it, unless he was a much more competent performer on rock than he frequently implied. Fortunately there is no need to battle with the chockstone, for on the right wall, at the same level, are much bigger and better hand and footholds which quickly lead to a little bilberry shelf. The grassy continuation ahead leads immediately below the last easy rocks to the summit of Loft Pike. Even getting my little dogs up this way involved no more than a quick yank on their collars.

Loft Crag and Gimmer Crag seen from Pike o'Stickle.

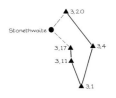

25 THE STONETHWAITE VALLEY SKYLINE

BEST MAP: *OS 1:25 000 Outdoor Leisure 4, North Western area*
APPROXIMATE TIME: *About 6 hours*
TERRAIN: *A twisting rocky climb, a pathless ascent on grass and a paddle across bogs lead to a battle with heather – but an excellent descent path. A good walk for a fine day* BUT DO NOT ATTEMPT IN POOR VISIBILITY.

ITINERARY	Book & Fell No	Height of ascent	Distance	Cumulative distance	Height above sea level	
		feet	miles	miles	feet	mtrs
STONETHWAITE					150	46
Eagle Crag	3.17	1300	2.00	2.00	1650	503
Sergeant's Crag	3.11	250	0.50	2.50	1873	571
High Raise	3.01	850	1.50	4.00	2500	762
Ullscarf	3.04	400	2.25	6.25	2370	726
Great Crag	3.20	200	2.75	9.00	1500	440
STONETHWAITE			1.50	10.50	150	46
Totals of heights and distances		3000	10.50			

This is one of the less obvious 'horseshoe rounds' highlighted by the map of Wainwright's ridges and my own first reaction was that it simply would not work. I was wrong. The ascent of Eagle Crag is superb and, despite two rather tedious stretches, the rest of the round has much of interest.

There are numerous parking places alongside the last stage of the road to Stonethwaite in Borrowdale (grid ref 263137) and from any of these just walk into the village. Then take the public bridleway (signed for Greenup Edge and Grasmere by the phone box), cross Stonethwaite Beck by the bridge, then turn south-east beside the beck, on a stony path below steep and wooded slopes on the left.

The view ahead is now completely dominated by the soaring rocky upthrust of Eagle Crag, aptly described by AW as a 'giant cornerstone', which splits Greenup Gill from Langstrath. Vertical crags around an arc of at least 180° seem to defend its summit and a first reaction is that they must be avoided by sneaking round behind them, either up Greenup Gill to the left or up Langstrath to the right. Ascent is possible by either of these

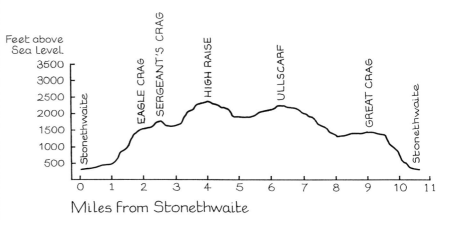

Miles from Stonethwaite

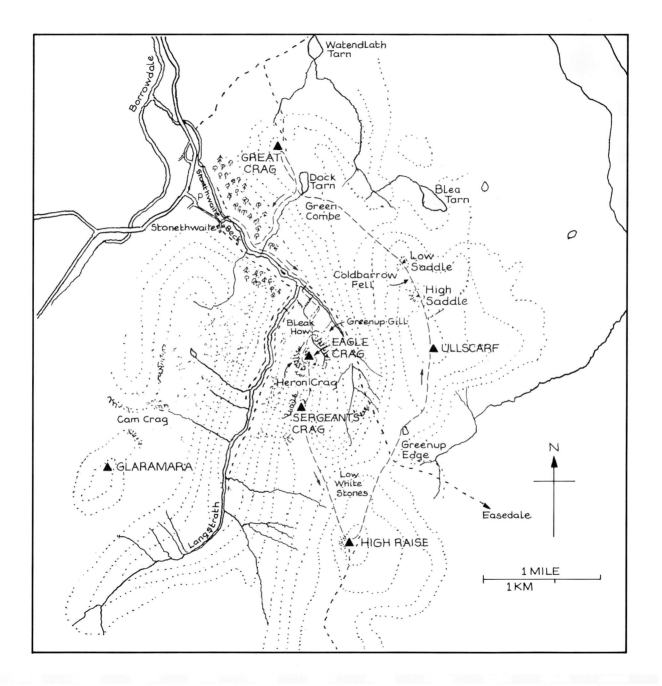

Watendlath
Tarn

Borrowdale

GREAT
CRAG

Dock
Tarn

Blea
Tarn

Green
Combe

Stonethwaite Beck

Stonethwaite

Low
Saddle

Coldbarrow
Fell

High
Saddle

Bleak
How

Greenup Gill

EAGLE
CRAG

ULLSCARF

Heron Crag

Cam Crag

SERGEANTS
CRAG

GLARAMARA

Greenup
Edge

Low
White
Stones

N

Langstrath

Easedale

HIGH RAISE

1 MILE

1 KM

dodging ways, particularly by grass slopes out of Greenup Gill, but that is a tedious and boring climb, better used as a descent, particularly in mist. However, a direct ascent – not 'direct' in the sense of the line taken by the falling drop of water but still 'up the front' – is perfectly possible for a normal fellwalker with the usual complement of legs and lungs. It presents a challenge because, seen head-on, it looks steep but it also promises some fine views. You will not be disappointed.

The path continues past the waterfalls of Galleny Force, more heard than seen from this bank, past a lovely pool at the very end of Langstrath Beck, from where there is a long-range view up Langstrath to Bowfell at its head, and then reaches a footbridge. Cross here and make as if to go up Langstrath but in only fifty paces or so turn left and cross a wire fence by a stile, continuing ahead over boggy ground but now on the west bank of the beck tumbling down Greenup Gill, keeping it on your left hand. Go through the gate in the wall ahead and continue beside the beck to the next wall, turning up alongside it and through a gateway (or a gap, for the wall is now falling down) and uphill beside it. Occasional pocket-steps shadow the wall to where what is left of it ends at a little crag. Cairns show the way now, slanting leftwards up grass and heading towards the vertical profile of Eagle Crag ahead, then turning right and more steeply uphill to where it meets a wall running up the main line of the ridge over the shoulder of Bleak How, which is now just a little lower.

Where this new wall meets a steep rock face a little higher up the slope, its last few feet are constructed of wooden palings rather than stones and it is easily crossed by a stile. Now an obvious broad and largely grassy shelf stretches upwards to the right, shortly reaching another shoulder, from where there is a good view up Langstrath. Immediately above this, the path turns left up a short gully with a couple of rock steps to arrive at a bay above. In this diagram for Eagle Crag 4, AW indicates a wooden fence spanning this gully, which he describes as the key to the ascent because of the two rock steps in it, but there is no sign now that there ever was such a fence and there is nothing to hinder this easy scramble. From the bay above, below more steep rock walls, AW points out that Eagle Crag can be seen by a short detour to the left and a narrow footpath which leads to a grand viewpoint for the vertical cliff, the site of some good rock-climbs.

Returning to the bay, below steep rocks where I stepped over the bones of a sheep that had found a short cut, the cairned way leads to the right, airily up more rock ledges and along grass shelves to a point almost overlooking a gully, with Sergeant's Crag now seen beyond it. Here the route turns uphill, zigzagging up easy rock steps and grass ledges to reach Eagle Crag's summit cairn which is perched on a tilted rock slab lying back from the edge of the high crags. When I arrived, on a sultry June day, it was surrounded by a cloud of infuriating midges. However, the rest of the walk ahead is now in view, while on the western arc many of the great Lakeland fells can be identified, from Scafell Pike to Skiddaw.

From Eagle Crag a path leads south to where there is a short descent at a wall-corner, without crossing the wall, then a peaty path continues in the same direction, shadowing the wall before trending away right across several small depressions to reach a rock spur thrown down by Sergeant's Crag. From here a glance back towards Eagle Crag gives no impression of the steep cliffs on its far flank; it just looks like a pile of blocks interspersed with grass ledges. From the nearby rocky summit there is a splendid view across Langstrath to the ice-scoured Cam Crag ridge and to Glaramara.

On seeing the steep rocks of Combe Head on Glaramara, I remembered clearly how,

Eagle Crag and the Stonethwaite Valley seen from Rosthwaite.

The ridge from Eagle Crag and Sergeant's Crag from High Raise.

some years ago, my little dog Freddie fell off those same rocks and into space. He fell an awfully long way and although he was alive when I reached him, I did not think he could possibly live. The femur on his right back leg had burst through his pelvic girdle with the impact of his fall. But he did survive and now, after an operation which left him with one leg shorter than the others, he runs happily all day long and has done so for about seven years since the fall. I wish I could do the same.

Just beyond Sergeant's Crag, the continuing path meets a wall reinforced by a fence to form a stile, but after it the path becomes fainter as it leads across grassy and feature-less fell towards a wide depression, en route for the highest land ahead which is High Raise. Beyond the depression there is no path, no cairns and nothing much but grass, although you turn the isolated rock outcrops of Long Crag and Low White Stones below them to the right. AW describes it as an easy climb of 850 feet but it feels like twice as much, a tedious ascent only relieved by crossing a stream at one point. Eventually the grass gives way to a scattering of boulders and here at last, the highest point on the circuit, is the trig point amongst them, together with two linked stone windbreaks. It is a logical place to rest awhile.

From the trig point a well-worn path heads north-east to a nearby metal fence-post on top of a clump of boulders, then turns north and follows a line of intermittent fence-posts to another group of rocks (Low White Stones) and then continues more steeply downhill on a boggy slope reminiscent of the Pennines, with bleached flat stones showing white against the black peat. The hause known as Greenup Edge, which is crossed by the Greenup Gill–Easedale path (the best way to escape back into Borrowdale in bad conditions), is quickly reached and left behind as the way continues along the line of fence-posts just east of north towards Ullscarf. But don't place too much reliance on the posts, as at one point they march through a singularly wet area where there are some very overgrown pools in the middle of boggy land. The path does try to dodge the worst of the ooze by keeping left of the posts for a short way, but with only partial success. When the land starts to rise again, the going greatly improves and a gentle climb over grass, still following the fence-posts, leads imperceptibly, interminably, to the summit cairn which is found amidst a few scattered rocks. On this ascent it might be good for morale to whistle a little tune perhaps, or sing 'Onward Christian Soldiers', or even think charitable thoughts about one's partner. AW describes the top of the fell as 'the dullest imaginable' and few would disagree, although there are higher hills to be seen in every direction except towards Windermere, so there are certainly some views. And with larks singing above and the knowledge that all is virtually downhill now, there are some consolations for attaining this point.

The line of old iron fence-posts leads on for a short way beyond the summit, then turns right (north-east) but at this point you lose any help from the fences and must keep straight on, heading north, on a faint footpath which soon leads to a cairn on the isolated rock outcrop of High Saddle. (Do not be confused by the new boundary fence marching towards Standing Crag or another new fence not shown on the OS map.) The faint path continues across the depression of Coldbarrow Fell towards more rocks on Low Saddle where there is another cairn. This is a fine viewpoint, with Blea Tarn and Watendlath Tarn seen, but a mile to the north-west Dock Tarn is also visible and just beyond that is the crumpled, rugged little summit of Great Crag, the last top of the day.

The path fizzles out now, but make a beeline over grass and past the occasional rock outcrop towards a cairned point that can be seen ahead, Green Combe. Before you reach it the easy grass gives way to tough heather and it is a tussle to reach the margin of Dock Tarn lying just below. A popular footpath from Watendlath goes along the west edge of the tarn and you could use it for a little way, but it is more in keeping with the rest of the walk to simply pick your own short route now along the grey rock on the highest land on the west side of the tarn to reach Great Crag's summit cairn.

Returning to the previously mentioned footpath, which is the only footpath here, follow it to the south-west down Willygrass Gill. The early part of the descent is particularly interesting, as it traces the line of the stream, since you can look across the valley for another good view of Eagle Crag and trace your upward route. The descent into the oak woods that follows is steep but the path is beautifully pitched and soon leads into the level meadows beside Stonethwaite Beck again and back to the start.

26 THE WATENDLATH CIRCUIT

BEST MAP: *OS 1:25 000 Outdoor Leisure 4, North Western area*
APPROXIMATE TIME: *4–5 hours*
TERRAIN: *Wet land, bog, a few stretches of blessedly dry ground.*

ITINERARY	Book & Fell No	Height of ascent	Distance	Cumulative distance	Height above sea level	
		feet	miles	miles	feet	mtrs
WATENDLATH					400	122
High Tove	3.16	800	1.00	1.00	1665	515
Armboth Fell	3.18	100	1.00	2.00	1570	479
Ullscarf	3.04	950	3.00	5.00	2370	726
Great Crag	3.20	200	2.75	7.75	1500	440
WATENDLATH			1.50	9.25	400	122
Totals of heights and distances		2050	9.25			

The high land between Thirlmere and Borrowdale is the wettest in the Lake District and the depth of the heather matched only by that 'back o' Skidda'. Progress is possible, however, on this bogtrotter's tramp and there is a certain grim satisfaction to be gained from having walked these fells.

The start is the attractive, isolated and sometimes over-popular hamlet of Watendlath in Borrowdale, about five miles south of Keswick. There is a good National Trust car park at the end of the road (grid ref 275163) and just at the entrance to this is a sign for 'Blea Tarn and Wythburn' pointing east alongside a beck and through a kissing-gate to a ford. The beck tumbles down Raise Gill and a causeway of stones zigzags up the steep slope to its south, ending at the top side of a little plantation where the intake wall turns south. There is a signpost here pointing south (right) for 'Wythburn and Blea Tarn' and another continuing ahead (east) up the slope for 'Armboth', and this is the way to go. A line of cairns leads up a long, grassy and often exceptionally boggy slope to reach a wire fence along the top of the ridge, with a kissing-gate and a large cairn just beyond it on the Thirlmere side.

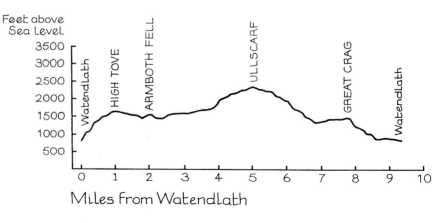

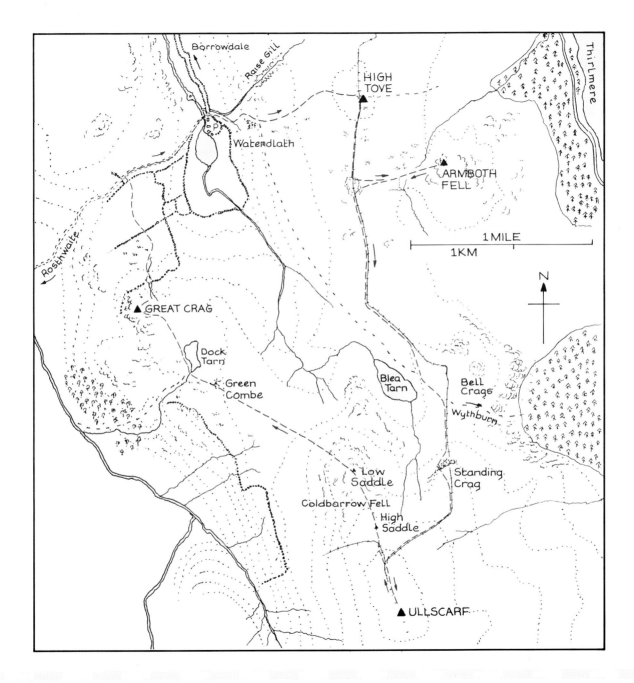

Borrowdale

Raise Gill

HIGH TOVE

Thirlmere

Watemdlath

ARMBOTH FELL

1 MILE

1 KM

Rosthwaite

N

GREAT CRAG

Dock Tarn

Green Combe

Blea Tarn

Bell Crags

Wythburn

Standing Crag

Low Saddle

Coldbarrow Fell

High Saddle

ULLSCARF

AW reckoned that 'It is hard to imagine that anybody feels any affection at all for High Tove' and he clearly did not feel much for Armboth Fell either, the next top, as, apart from 'peak-baggers … other walkers may justifiably consider its ascent a waste of precious time'. A further complication is that the OS map marks a vague area to the ENE of High Tove as 'Armboth Fell' whereas AW is quite clear that it is the small rocky area to the south-east (spot height 479m on the map) which is lower in altitude than High Tove. To reach Armboth Fell it is probably as well to continue south along the line of the boundary fence to the firmer ground of Middle Crag, then remember that today you are a peak-bagger, take a deep breath and steer a course due east towards it. 'Avoid a bad bog in the depression' (on the way to Armboth Fell) is AW's good advice; then retrace your steps towards Middle Crag and return as soon as possible to the boundary fence along the watershed, paddling your way along beside it and wishing you were wearing your wellies until Blea Tarn comes into view. A short diversion to Bell Crags on the left may be worth making as, for once, there is some solid rock to scramble on; I guarantee you will leave wet footprints. There are remains of a small quarry here and also a surprisingly large, square sheepfold below the crags.

The next bit of dry land in view is the prominent Standing Crag to the south, so resume marching beside the boundary fence which heads straight for its steepest rocks. You will have to dodge either right or left to get round this obstacle but can then pick up the line of the fence again at the top of Standing Crag and follow it up gentle, grassy and, thankfully, much drier slopes. When the fence itself ends, a line of old iron fence-posts continues the direction just a little further before turning left (south) and leading to the cairn on the summit of Ullscarf, piled amidst a few scattered rocks. As what is considered to be the most central of Lakeland's fells above two thousand feet in altitude it is rather uninspiring but, like Everest, it is there.

Reverse steps along the line of old fence-posts, this time heading north, but when the posts turn right (north-east) you continue straight ahead on a faint footpath to a cairn on the isolated rock outcrop of High Saddle. (Do not be confused by a new fence not shown on the OS map.) The footpath continues across the depression of Coldbarrow Fell to another cairn amongst more rocks on Low Saddle, which is a fine viewpoint for Blea Tarn and the terrain ahead. Dock Tarn can be seen about a mile to the north-west and beyond it the numerous little outcrops of the last top of the day, Great Crag.

Just south-east of Dock Tarn is one more little high point, Green Combe, crowned by an obvious cairn, thus making it a natural point at which to aim in the steady descent from Low Saddle since it remains in sight when the tarn is out of sight. But if you think it is all going to be a doddle from here on, you are in for a surprise for the easy grass gives way to luxuriant heather and numerous small battles have to be fought with it to reach the cairn. You still have a tussle to descend to the margin of Dock Tarn where at least, on its western edge, is a good footpath. This is worth using, going north along the edge

The hamlet of Watendlath and its tarn, seen from just below Great Crag.

of this reedy but attractive tarn and for about 500 yards beyond its north edge. A tall 'finger-post' of rock beside the path then marks one point (although there are others) where a faint trod may be used to scramble through deep heather to locate the nearby summit cairn on Great Crag. Its greatness is hardly in its size, but in its wonderfully wild setting.

Retrace your steps to the path, and the route home is now easy as it leads (north) downhill to a gate through a wall, then posts waymark the route round a conservation area of bog to another gate at a fence. A firm path now leads pleasantly to a gate at the edge of the popular Rosthwaite track and a right turn here soon returns you to Watendlath. You'll be lucky if you have dry feet and after saying at the very beginning that this is a very wet walk, anyone who doesn't have dry shoes etc. to change into is a Wally.

ITINERARY	Book & Fell No	Height of ascent	Distance	Cumulative distance	Height above sea level	
		feet	miles	miles	feet	mtrs
AMBLESIDE					250	76
Loughrigg Fell	3.27	1050	2.50	2.50	1101	335
Silver How	3.24	950	2.50	5.00	1292	395
Blea Rigg	3.14	650	2.00	7.00	1776	541
Sergeant Man	3.02	700	1.50	8.50	2414	736
High Raise	3.01	140	0.50	9.00	2500	762
Ullscarf	3.04	400	2.25	11.25	2370	726
Armboth Fell	3.18	250	3.00	14.25	1570	479
High Tove	3.16	200	1.00	15.25	1665	515
High Seat	3.09	300	1.00	16.25	1995	608
Bleaberry Fell	3.10	150	1.25	17.50	1932	590
Walla Crag	3.25	170	1.25	18.75	1234	379
KESWICK			2.50	21.25	250	76
Totals of heights and distances		4960	21.25			

27 THE SPINE OF THE CENTRAL FELLS (a traverse)

BEST MAP: *OS 1:50000 Landranger 90 Penrith, Keswick & Ambleside area. At 1:25000 scale, Outdoor Leisure maps 7, 6 and 4 are all needed.*
APPROXIMATE TIME: *10–11 hours*
TERRAIN: *Good paths on the first half of the walk, diabolically wet ones thereafter.*

This fine traverse of eleven tops is a challenge to fellwalkers as, apart from the length of the walk, it includes some of the boggiest ground in the Lakes and also some of the most complex. You will never keep your boots dry, so you may as well wear trainers and not worry about wet feet. On the basis that it is better to deal with the intricacies first, while you are fresh, this walk begins in Ambleside.

Wherever you park in Ambleside, the tall elegant spire of St Mary's Church can usually be seen and the lane immediately north of it leads into and across Rothay Park to cross the River Rothay at Miller Bridge. Turn right at the side road beyond and then left up the first metalled road, which rises to Brow Head Farm. The road becomes a track as it kinks back to the right above the farm and leads through some woodland on Miller Brow, passing the old club house of the former Ambleside Golf Club, then up a wide walled lane to reach a gate and open fell. Just ahead and slightly downhill (south-west) is a broad hause, a junction of several paths where there is also a tiny but permanent tarn (shown on the OS 1:25 000 map). However, only one path heads uphill to the north-west, and that, of course, is the one you need. It climbs steadily, with a short passage over

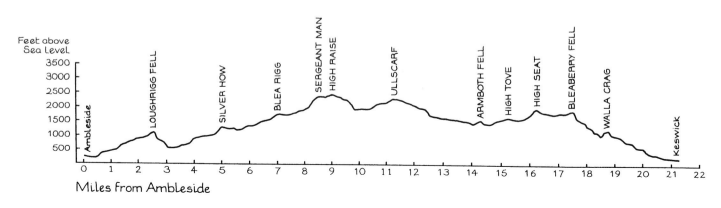

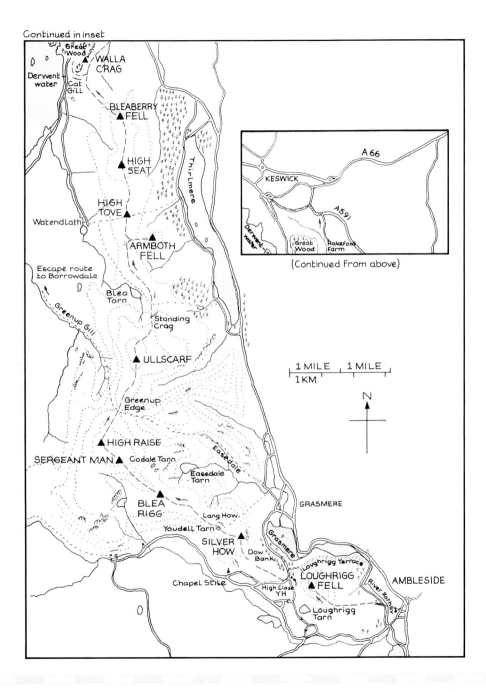

Continued in inset

Great
Wood

WALLA
CRAG

Derwent
water

Cat
Gill

BLEABERRY
FELL

HIGH
SEAT

Thirlmere

HIGH
TOVE

Watendlath

ARMBOTH
FELL

Escape route
to Borrowdale

Greenup Gill

BLEA
TARN

Standing
Crag

ULLSCARF

Greenup
Edge

HIGH RAISE

SERGEANT MAN   Codale Tarn

Easedale
Tarn

Easedale

GRASMERE

BLEA
RIGG

Lang How

Youdell Tarn

SILVER
HOW

Dow
Bank

Grasmere

Loughrigg Terrace

LOUGHRIGG
FELL

AMBLESIDE

Chapel Stile

High Close
YH

Loughrigg
Tarn

River Rothay

1 MILE   1 MILE

1 KM

N

A 66

KESWICK

A591

Derwent
water

Great
Wood

Rakefoot
Farm

(Continued from above)

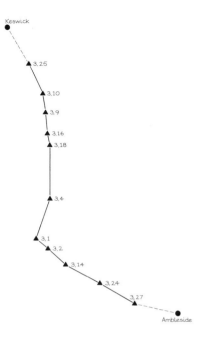

rocks but otherwise over grass and bracken, to a point where Loughrigg Tarn comes into sight below on the left. An undulating and well-cairned path continues to a fairly steep slope at the head of a depression and immediately beyond it is the summit trig on Loughrigg Fell. As the highest point on a miniature mountain range surrounded by many other mountains, it is rightly famed as a viewpoint.

The next top is Silver How, the way to it being partly masked by woods, so I suggest the easiest way is to take the well-used descent path to the north-west, towards Grasmere and with lovely views over the lake. Turn left at Loughrigg Terrace, near the foot of the fell, and keep left when the Grasmere – Skelwith Bridge road is reached until it forks. Bear right here, up to and round the sharp corner beside High Close Youth Hostel until, immediately beyond it, it is possible to escape onto open fell again. A path leads round into a shallow grassy valley and near its head you must turn left, west, across boggy ground to follow an obvious path rising up a little escarpment opposite. There is a tiny tarn on the shelf above.

The twisting and turning is now largely over as the grassy path undulates over Dow Bank and other little high points of land to another junction where a popular path crosses from Grasmere to Chapel Stile. Cross this, and trend rightwards, north, up a short, open gully to an easing of the gradient where there is a big cairn. A good path continues along the top edge of the wooded slopes running down to Rydal Water and

Looking from Silver How along the ridge towards Sergeant Man.

The broad ridge south of Blea Rigg.

Grasmere to reach a cairn on the pleasant grassy top of Silver How. There is now just one change of direction, to the west, on a reasonable path along the broad top of the ridge to reach Youdell Tarn, the biggest of three tarns here, beneath the little crag of Lang How and usually colonised by black-headed gulls. A busy footpath from Easedale also joins the ridge at this point and the combined trod now continues, winding along the crest.

You can stride out confidently on the clear paths along this broad ridge with some grand views to Easedale on the right. You will probably walk past the rocky high point of Blea Rigg without realising it and then your main impression will be of a gradual rise to a point where the ridge itself narrows and Codale Tarn can be seen on the Easedale side of the ridge. A last climb leads up to the small conical top of Sergeant Man.

Unusually for a ridge, the next objective, which is High Raise, is out of sight but you should be able to pick up a line of iron fence-posts leading to the north-west, with a path beside them, which soon passes over a swelling of land, past an evil black tarn and so to the scattering of boulders, two windbreaks and the trig point on its top. For the first time, the northern half of the Lake District fills the scene ahead. More fence-posts lead to the north, down the boggy slope to the hause of Greenup Edge, crossed by the Greenup Gill–Easedale path. This could give an escape down to Borrowdale on the left but the fence-posts, wavering in their course as they pick a way around bogs and through pools, continue to the north towards Ullscarf, and the footpath follows their line.

Be thankful for the posts, as there are few other features on this rolling grassy moor to give it the distinction, as AW said, of probably being the most central of the Lakeland fells above two thousand feet. That distinction is counterbalanced by another: Ullscarf's grassy top is 'the dullest imaginable'. At least it is easy going now underfoot. A few more fence-posts continue northwards beyond the summit, then swing north-east to a junction with a newer fence on a rock outcrop. It is no longer a 'ruined' fence but one

Harrison Stickle and Pavey Ark seen from Silver How.

in good repair and it leads confidently to the bold outcrop of Standing Crag, from where there is a good view to Blea Tarn, below.

Down the slope beyond lies the most saturated land for miles, but it still cannot begin to match miles of the Pennine Way for bogs and peat groughs and you'll find it quite easy going, just sticking beside the fence. You cross the Wythburn–Watendlath path, usually identified more by a line of longitudinal puddles than a firm trod, then the fence continues along the 'top' of the ridge. The solid rocks of Bell Crags loom up ahead but

Skiddaw seen from the summit of High Raise.

the fence swings away and continues squelching north, thankfully passing over firmer ground on Middle Crag. To the east of this is Armboth Fell (spot height 479m on the map) and although AW was very definite that it is not worth visiting, he still included it as a top on the ridge-line, so you had better just paddle over there. Then return and award yourself some Brownie points for not shirking the job.

It is time to start singing jolly songs now for just a little further north and still beside the fence (just think of the chaps who had to build the fence and that will cheer you up!) is the eighth top (after you have visited Armboth Fell) of High Tove. Its large cairn is near to a gate in the fence used by a path crossing from Watendlath to Thirlmere, but don't consider sneaking off to Watendlath. Just scoff another Mars Bar, check that your feet have not become webbed and press on, because you are definitely winning.

Continue gently uphill, still beside the fence, to reach High Seat which is quite a good viewpoint. It has a trig point, on dry ground, near a rock knoll named Man and a path leads down from here to Ashness Bridge, which will be infested with tourists so you will be able to avoid them and have a good laugh at AW's description of the next bit, to Bleaberry Fell, as 'a walk to wish on one's worst enemy, especially after rain'.

Bleaberry Fell, at last, marks the end of the squelch. The views towards Derwentwater are very good and the ground underfoot becomes much firmer as an obvious path marks a descent to the north-west, curving downhill to a little outcrop where there is a lonely sheepfold. Gentle grassy slopes then lead to the head of Cat Gill, contouring round the head of the ravine to Walla Crag. This is a delightful rock escarpment, its top clothed in heather, its tree-clad slopes overlooking Derwentwater. You may even have enough energy left to enjoy it.

All that remains is to descend to the valley. One way is to return to the head of Cat Gill and follow the well-used path down into Great Wood, where the National Trust car park is a good pick-up point (grid ref 272213); you would save a little under three miles doing this. Alternatively, use the footpath along the continuation of Walla Crag to the north-east to Rakefoot Farm, from whence a good minor road leads to the A591 as it begins its last descent to Keswick. Well done! You'll look back on this walk with pride.

INDEX

Fell names in CAPITALS are the subjects of chapters in
Wainwright's *Pictorial Guides to the Lakeland Fells*

Page numbers in *italics* refer to illustrations